WHY YOUR WEALTH MANAGER IS ROBBING YOU BLIND

WHY YOUR WEALTH MANAGER IS ROBBING YOU BLIND

3 Simple Ways To Finally Start To Beat Your Market Benchmark

Frustrated with your underperforming portfolio and the never-ending excuses from your financial advisor?

LANE CLARK

Why Your Wealth Manager Is Robbing You Blind

ISBN: 979-8-89694-784-4 - eBook

ISBN: 979-8-89694-785-1 - Paperback

FOREWORD FROM THE AUTHOR:

Beating your market benchmark consistently isn't easy, but it isn't as hard as we're led to believe. In this book I have tried to condense two and a half decades of trading experience into a couple of hundred pages. If it helps just one investor, then it will have been time well spent for me. However, deep down, I hope it will assist many more.

I love the world of wealth management, but it needs to be modernised. Investors are craving better performance and lower fees.

I hope this book can become your investment toolbox that you can turn to at any time to assist you on your journey to build a benchmark beating portfolio.

Also, I just want to take this opportunity to thank my business partner Ed Davies for putting up with me for as long as he has, and I look forward to another decade (or two) working with you in our mission to try and change how the world invests.

I'd also like to thank everyone who has ever invested with me, and for the shareholders of our business who have placed immense trust in Ed and I to build an industry changing investment vehicle.

Finally, thank you to my gorgeous wife Emma and my two brilliant children, Lexi and Sophia. Life without you three by my side wouldn't be half as fun, and I probably wouldn't know what to do with myself when I'm not working! One thing is for sure though: I'd be a lot richer.

Thank you guys.

Table of Contents

IMPORTANT
THE PROBLEM THIS BOOK SOLVES (READ THIS FIRST!)

As an investor, you are probably used to performing below your market benchmark. You've perhaps been frustrated for years or maybe even decades with your wealth manager and Independent Financial Advisor (IFA). You wonder why they consistently fail to beat your market benchmark, and please: don't even get me started on their fees!

You've considered taking your portfolio from their custody and taking control of it yourself, but either from a lack of time, or a couple of mistimed initial gambits; you've changed track.

Potentially you reverted to what you've always done. You're back with the same old model; high fees, under performance and a plethora of excuses.

If this is resonating, then let me inform you right now:

This book is for you.

In fact, purchasing this book might become the best investment decision you've made for quite some time.

As you're about to find out, this book delivers when it comes to assisting you to beat your market benchmark, and your years of underperformance are probably coming closer to ending than you realise.

Not only that, once we start explaining the three techniques and frameworks that can be utilised to beat your market benchmark consistently, you will be arming yourself with the confidence that these same techniques have also been utilised by hundreds (perhaps thousands) of investors globally. They're not frameworks and approaches designed for the elite hedge fund manager who has an understanding perhaps on a far more advanced plane than yours.

They've worked the whole gamut: from people and investors who were relatively new to the investment game, to seasoned pros. From electricians to business owners, to athletes, to individuals in high flying corporate roles, and many other industries in between. No territory or investor has been left uncovered!

The ideas outlined have already generated market-beating returns for both myself, my business partner Ed (Edward Davies) and clients in 15 different countries (and growing) globally.

The reality is that the wealth management model as we know it isn't (IS NOT) designed to 'beat market benchmarks' for investors.

How can it be when the money that is handed over from investors is merely linked to global stock markets and other lower yielding asset classes?

After the wealth managers and IFAs have taken their regular management and performance fees, then the only question is, how much less performance than your market benchmark did you achieve? More on this later.

The current status quo isn't good enough, and if this book makes investors pause and realise there are other ways to invest, then its purpose is served.

We're bred to believe that using the traditional wealth manager/financial advisor model is the only way to invest, however the reality is that it's the institutions managing the money that want us to believe that myth.

Why wouldn't they if they'll earn a 1.5 percent management fee on their 150 billion pounds that they manage, regardless of how your portfolio performs. Talking of 1.5 percent fees, if that's all your wealth manager has been charging you, then you're one of the luckier ones.

There are many wealth managers and IFAs out there who charge substantially more than this and come the end of the year, the outcome is the same: Underperformance. This book could shift this dynamic for you.

As well as the three market beating techniques you can employ to outperform your market benchmark, this book will also:

- Show you how to build a portfolio that many investors have replicated to regularly beat their market benchmarks and in some cases by more than 1.5 x per annum.

- The amazing secrets and frameworks of how to build a portfolio that is diversified, robust and aims to perform regardless of the market climate.

- It will show you why the 'one tactic' used by *all* financial advisors is destined to fail year after year after year.

- The techniques and frameworks demonstrated in this book have already been utilised successfully by investors globally, and we will demonstrate exactly how to replicate this model with your investment portfolio.

- It will place you into a position whereby you can take any market related decisions away from your wealth manager or IFA. In other words, it will help you to gain control, and to build your wealth.

The strategies, techniques and frameworks explained have also been traded through every recent volatile market condition;

The Credit Crunch, COVID-19 pandemic, Global wars, The Trump Tariffs.

Regardless of market climate, they have delivered.

However, before we go further, these strategies and methods of investing are not your 'investing magic wand'. They will not always be right every day, week or month. There will be periods where they're occasionally wrong. However, year on year, we expect they will deliver for you.

It's important that you stay in the game, do not take on too much risk, and on the back of this, find a methodology that can beat your market benchmark consistently.

Ed and I have operated as market-beating traders for over two decades each, but the strategies and techniques aren't designed exclusively for people like us.

They're being used globally by advocates at this very moment in time. The movement we have been building is beginning to build traction and momentum.

Regarding the strategies, apart from the elite techniques employed, there are numerous other key reasons why I expect that they will assist you to change how you invest moving forward:

THEY WORK QUICKLY. Unlike working with your financial advisor who rolls out the underperformance excuse at the conclusion of every year, you'll be able to notice the market beating difference within a quarter or two.

NO MORE HIGH FEES. Wealth managers like to charge management fees, performance fees, fund fees, transaction fees, redemption fees. That's a lot of fees. However, the strategies outlined and employed in this book are low cost and will assist you to migrate away from the high-cost wealth management structure indefinitely.

THEY ARE TIMELESS. The strategies we will outline for you will only invest in global stock markets. They do not explore any 'arbitrage situations' that potentially operate well for a few years and then embark on a disastrous run. These are strategies and frameworks that will work effectively regardless of the climate. Leave the fads and the 'get rich quick' schemes to the people who sell 'how to trade' courses!

THEY WORK FOR INVESTORS LARGE AND SMALL. Whether you hold a 15k GBP portfolio or a 1.5M GBP portfolio, we can provide the outline and frameworks to the strategies that will help you beat your market benchmark, and as your portfolio and wealth grows, so will your exposure to these strategies.

Before pushing forward with this book, please understand this:

Changing how you have invested for perhaps decades won't be easy. You need to understand that and be committed to the process.

It's been bred into us that the only way to invest is to let the overpaid wealth managers do it for us. You need to accept there are other ways, and there are most certainly better ways.

If you believe you want to make this change enough, and you are prepared to offer 100 percent commitment to this, this book can become your toolbox for market success.

However, if you are of the opinion that overnight, you're going to turn an underperforming portfolio into one that will double your money every year, then I'll be candid: this book probably isn't for you.

Sorry if that offends you, but the reality is this; there is no silver bullet, or magic wand to market beating performance.

There are so called 'gurus' out there right now, that inform people that they can teach them how to trade and invest successfully in minutes. I'm telling you right now as an experienced market participant, they can't.

Leave the dreaming to the dreamers.

The reason I believe it is important to state this at this very moment in time is because if you're not the right fit, if you do not possess the right aptitude for learning, and aren't open minded, then I could probably save you a number of hours and suggest you put this book down right now.

I know it's strange (perhaps even a little weird) to attempt to put people off reading this book further, but I am incredibly motivated to change how people invest, but you need to want to make that change.

I want to help people who want to make that change and are prepared to make the modifications to their portfolio structures that are required.

I can lead you to the water, but you need to learn how to drink it for yourself.

What you need to understand is how passionate I am regarding my mission. You need to know that if you're not 100 percent committed to making this work, that no matter how wise some of my words might be, they'll be useless.

However, if you're reading this introduction and are thinking that what I am saying echoes your frustrations and dreams, then this book could become your most valuable investment tool.

If you are ready to commit, are keen to take on board what I'm telling you, and modify your stale and outdated portfolio structure, then you can build a market benchmark beating portfolio. You can change how you invest forever.

However, before we delve deeper. Why am I doing this?

If you commit to this book and the techniques within it, at some stage on your investment transformational journey you'll realise exactly how valuable this book is to you. In fact, depending on your portfolio size, it could be worth tens of thousands of GBP to you, or perhaps hundreds of thousands of GBP. If that's the case, you might be wondering why would

I provide these trade secrets and frameworks to you for such a low entry point/price?

Let me answer that and address the massive elephant in the room.

In fact, the answer is pretty damn simple. Alongside my business partner, I founded a very successful wealth tech platform called TPP (www.tppglobal.io). I have the honour of working with investors globally and helping them to beat their market benchmarks year in and year out.

Whether it's an old friend from school, a family member, an entrepreneur, or an athlete I have met on this journey, I am proud to say I have assisted them.

However, despite this and the fact that since our founding, word of mouth has spread into so many countries that I'm losing count, I know it's impossible that we can ever service everyone.

However, if I can educate people and show them how you CAN beat your market benchmark and show them there is a different way, then the investment world will become a better place.

Investment managers shouldn't be allowed to charge what they charge for the performance (or lack of) they deliver, and if it takes an insider like me to open your eyes to this, the investment world will be left in a better state whether you decide to work with us or strike it out alone.

You'll always be told it's too hard to build a winning structure without paying for the expertise, but today, I will show you that it's a lot simpler than you probably ever imagined.

One thing is for sure, if anyone who reads this book decides to work with TPP, then we look forward to it, but my main goal is to give back and show people that it's time to take control, it's time to empower yourself, and it's time to beat your market benchmark consistently without the reliance on your financial advisor and their excessive fee structure.

Even if you read and digest this book and continue to operate how you have been, but you manage to negotiate a better fee structure with your wealth manager, then again; my mission here is complete.

Whatever you extract from this book, and whatever route your journey veers towards, your investment performance should improve, and you should end up paying substantially less fees than you currently do.

A win for you, and a win for the industry.

The wealth management world has provided Ed and I with great careers, but it is ready and ripe for disruption, and we hope this movement we are creating and this book you are reading is another step towards this.

Are you ready to beat your market benchmark?

Let's do this. Thank you very much for providing me with the opportunity to show you how.

Sincerely
Lane Clark

Ps: When you read this for the first couple of times, read it from cover to cover. Then in the future, utilise it as an investing toolbox that you can revert to when the occasion permits. We all need effective tools in our armour; after all knowledge is always power or equates with power.

WHY THIS BOOK IS POTENTIALLY MORE IMPORTANT NOW THAN EVER BEFORE (THE WEALTH MANAGEMENT WORLD IS CHANGING, BE AHEAD OF THIS EVOLUTION):

I am not one to go down the route of dramatisation or hyperbole for the sake of it. I won't make a comment or a statement for 'click bait', and most of what I say, and state will be based on statistics and facts.

So, let's start with a shocking one:

A well-known fact is that over 80 percent of active wealth managers underperform a simple market tracker each and every year.

To add a little context, in an industry where many of the world's brightest minds reside, we cannot manage to build funds that can beat a market tracker.

If this wasn't enough, in the UK alone, we pay more than 150m GBP per year, for this underperformance in fees.

I know, it is absolutely ridiculous!

In fact, I'm embarrassed stating those figures for an industry that I love and have grown up around.

I almost feel that on behalf of the world of wealth management that I need to apologise to every investor out there.

Sorry.

So why is it so bad? How can an industry which contributes a large proportion of GDP for every major country and economy perform so badly for its investors, and why hasn't anyone ever done anything about it previously?

The problem isn't the people within the industry, it certainly isn't the skillsets, the lack of brain power or the IQ. Trust me, there are plenty of brilliant minds within this space.

It's because the wealth management model is stale, outdated and antiquated.

If wealth managers and financial advisors focused on the outcome for their investors; the industry would be incredibly different.

However, the model isn't designed to do that.

It's a big statement to make, but I am certainly prepared to do so.

By working with a financial advisor or wealth manager in the current stale and outdated wealth management model, it is almost *impossible* to beat your market benchmark, and I will tell you exactly why later in this book.

Change is needed, where shareholder profit isn't the number one priority for these companies, and being able to consistently beat your market benchmark yearly becomes the norm.

If you have the ability to consistently outperform your market benchmark and grow your wealth year in and year out, there are very few problems in your world that you won't be able to find a solution for.

Most investors start off by doing what their father did, and what his father did before him; handing over their money blindly to a financial advisor with the justification of it's just what 'we' do…

However, if you've ever taken the time to analyse their model and realised how they allocate your assets, you probably already wonder what exactly you're paying for.

Most IFAs have never placed a trade in the markets in their lifetime, yet you entrust them with your wealth.

It's a harsh truth but most (not all) IFAs are merely salesmen dressed up as a 'financial expert'. Apologies to the good ones.

As an investor, maybe when working with one of these 'professionals', you've managed to get lucky. You perhaps timed your entry after a large market pullback, or you've persisted with it for long enough to make some sort of return. However, with inflation factored in, is anyone truly content with that relationship?

You don't need to answer that as it's a rhetorical question.

Along the way, many investors have tried to figure it out for themselves, but at the end of the day they all have their own careers to prioritise, and families to support. Your investment's structure probably takes a back seat, unfortunately.

It shouldn't.

Having a solid portfolio structure in place will improve your life.

What's the difference between an investor who makes less than their market benchmark every year, and an investor who beats their benchmark consistently?

The difference isn't the wealth manager you work with. The difference is the few simple tweaks that this book will assist you to make to your portfolio structure that will change how you invest forever.

Luckily for you, this book will provide the exact learnings, findings and expensive mistakes made by market beating traders over the decades and put them into simple to follow guidelines for you.

These guidelines and frameworks have been used to turn underperforming portfolios ranging from 15,000 GBP to multiple millions, into portfolios that have been generating north of 20 percent per annum consistently. Yes, just to confirm, you did read that figure right!

After implementing some simple modifications and structures into your portfolio, you'll witness within a matter of months how these revolutionary tactics and frameworks will turbo charge your wealth.

In other words, you'll evolve from a mindset of never understanding why your wealth manager consistently underperforms and having to listen to their never-ending excuses year after year, to building a portfolio that beats your benchmark consistently and in some cases by at least 1.5 x per annum.

By the way, I haven't implemented these game changing tactics to just a mere handful of investors on my journey. I have personally implemented these tactics with hundreds of investors around the globe (our company likewise) and changed how they have invested forever.

In the process, I have found out what works best, the pitfalls to avoid, and any investor I have worked with has built a better portfolio through the experience.

Best of all, *all* of these trade secrets and tactics are within this book.

Let me conclude this small chapter by stating that the world of wealth management is evolving. Bit by bit, change is coming. In the years to come I expect there will be a number of market beating solutions as the world wakes up and wonders why we all accepted this model for as many decades as we did. However, now is your opportunity to be part of this change, to be on the right side of the curve.

In years to come, the IFA will become like the travel agent. We'll wonder why we ever used them.

After reading and absorbing this book, you'll be on course to make this change and evolution alongside the earlier adopters. You'll be ready to consistently outperform your market index.

THINK LIKE A WORLD CLASS INVESTOR AND BILLIONAIRE (CREATE THE WINNING MINDSET) … …

If you want to become wealthier, you must think and act like someone with a winning and wealthy mindset.

Again, if you are reading this book and hoping to find the holy grail of investing where you'll make 100 percent per year each and every year, allow me to let you down gently straight away.

This is not going to happen.

If you've heard of these day traders making 2 percent every day and are secretly hoping we'll show you how to do the same, let me disappoint you once again.

This isn't going to happen.

I've worked in the industry for over two decades and I've never met a successful day trader. I've met traders who have informed me about a stunning trade, month, quarter or even a year.

However, someone who has managed to achieve this type of epic results year in and year out? I've never met one.

Seriously though, if you know one, send them my details, we'd love to showcase them on TPP.

If you've watched some of these YouTube adverts where so called 'traders' will teach you how to trade and you'll generate 5 percent per month following this methodology of theirs, again this isn't going to happen.

If anyone ever informs you that they can double your money in a year, or even make 40-50 percent per annum, they are either lying, or they're taking excessive risk.

The bad news is this, at some stage following a methodology like this will end in tears. Something will go wrong. It is only a matter of time. I would love to dress this up, and let you know that there are traders and investors who can do this. However, it is a hard-hitting fact that this type of risk management isn't sustainable. Run as far as you can from promises and performance like this.

This brings us back to mindset. Real investors, real wealthy individuals know that 'overnight success' stories don't happen. They might look like they have, but the reality is, the hard yards and preparation has taken place for quite some time beforehand.

So please, from here on in adopt the mindset of a successful market beating investor, or a billionaire, not a mindset of somebody who wants to generate 500 percent in one year.

When I say 'billionaire' I don't mean someone who has inherited their wealth or their billions like Paris Hilton (apologies for the name drop Paris). Or someone who has achieved very little to earn their wealth. I'm talking about the 'self-made' billionaire, the person who at one stage was just like you.

To think like one of these billionaires or even a successful market beating investor, you must first understand the choices they make in life and in business. How they have shaped their beliefs.

For decades I have studied this group of people from working with them and studying from afar. They all share one thing in common:

They all seem to invest in as many 'sure thing assets' as they can. They are constantly looking to minimise risk, whilst providing themselves with a positive return. They also compound their returns.

In fact, the recently retired Warren Buffett says it best. This is a famous quote of his that you might be familiar with:

"The first rule of an investment is do not lose (money). And the second rule of an investment is don't forget the first rule."

Making solid, steady and market beating returns is your key to long term wealth. Compounding your returns is how you build the wealth you desire. I'll explain more on this topic later, and it is key.

When we look to recruit world class and elite market beating traders for our platform, we don't look for superheroes; traders and investors who have showed us the track record of the *one* year they accrued 120 percent or the *one* time they returned 5 times their market benchmark.

If anything, this talk would scare Ed and I.

We look for investors and traders who consistently outperform. We look for individuals and teams who know how to manage volatility, who understand when to cut a loss, who don't take on excessive risk or leverage, and instead: they focus on grinding away profits year on year.

For all I know, you might already have this mindset. My experience of working with successful individuals over the decades in a variation of different industries informs me that the mindset might already be in place. Only the tools have been missing.

This book will provide you with the tools and the guidance.

However, if you are known to take on too much risk, to push the boat out that little bit more, then may I ask you to taper down that mentality.

It might serve you for the short term, but over the mid and long term, this mentality will make you go bust.

The keys to beating your market benchmark are to build a methodology that works consistently and for you to stay in the game/in the market at all times. The only thing that can stop the latter is if you take on too much risk.

Trust me, this situation never ends well.

Start developing the mindset of a winner. A billionaire, a world class investor. Take the wins, manage your risk, accept a reasonable level of volatility, manage your expectations, and outperform each and every year.

It will be the difference between turning your 250,000 GBP into multiple millions over the next decade and a half or losing it all and ending the dream after one risk too many. Please trust me on this.

If you're constantly checking your investment account or are pressing refresh on your trading app; YOU ARE TAKING ON TOO MUCH RISK.

Act like a billionaire, build the structure, trust the process, and let the methodology you implement make you money.

Let me ask you a question; Does the below resemble you, is it how you think, can you relate to it?

What do I want? (Hopes, dreams and desires)

I want solid returns on my investment structure:

I want a clear and proven investment strategy that forecasts impressive profits.

I want to sustain (and hopefully improve) the annual returns I'm currently getting from my wealth manager, whilst paying less on fees.

I want low-risk investments:

Whilst I am looking at steady gains, I don't want to start making speculative investments or following a high-risk market strategy.

I want to stop paying over-priced fees to a wealth manager:

Given the market over the past 18 months, I'm making significantly smaller gains from my investments. Hence, I don't want to keep paying a 1.5 percent fee on my portfolio.

I want the advice, guidance and investment strategy quality that I get from a wealth manager, but without the overpriced fees.

I want my wealth manager to reduce their fees in the current market and provide a lot more value otherwise I will look at leaving.

I need a strong client relationship with whoever is managing my portfolio:

I want updates on the state of my investments and always kept in the loop.

I want to have transparency and trust with whoever is managing my investments.

I want a personalised service… Whether that is with a wealth fund manager or new technologies, I want an investment strategy that is personalised to my investment goals, the size of my portfolio and preferences.

I need to be confident that the group I am about to work with understands my unique financial situation.

What about this?

But what do I *really* want? I want very strong market benchmark beating returns without significant risks, without paying the overpriced fees I'm currently paying my wealth and fund manager.

What outside forces do I believe have prevented my best life?

For a long time, I have been locked into a traditional model of the wealth manager and there hasn't been the option to get a similar style of service with lower fees.

I don't have the time to properly learn these investment strategies and manage my investments the best way possible.

What are my prejudices?

With new technologies and being an early adopter there comes increased risk.

Investment technologies have not been around long enough, and I don't believe A.I. is developed enough to handle my portfolio.

Wealth managers are more concerned with getting my fee to pay for their lavish lifestyle than actually growing my portfolio.

My biggest pain points are…

I am frustrated by over-priced fees…

My wealth manager charges an annual management fee of 1.5 percent, which has significantly eroded my investment over the past few years.

In a bull market I'm frustrated because a percentage of my gains are being eroded by my manager fees. In a bear market I'm still paying 1 percent of my portfolio to someone who is responsible for a portfolio that just keeps shrinking.

I'm tired of having to pay additional fees for transactions, performance and sometimes for additional advice.

I am frustrated by poor communication:

I don't receive regular updates from my wealth manager on my investments (especially when the market is going down and I'm losing money!).

I can't get in touch with my wealth manager when I have questions or concerns about the state of the market or my investments. There have been instances where this inability to reach my manager has cost me thousands when they didn't sell quickly enough.

I often get treated like an idiot and that I couldn't possibly understand the 'high-level' investment strategy that is a closely guarded secret. I almost feel like my portfolio is being held hostage.

I am frustrated by poor performance:

I have lost tens, hundreds of thousands of pounds over the past year and a half, or when markets haven't increased in a straight line.

I'm not getting value anymore from my wealth manager when my portfolio is shrinking and yet they still charge me 1.5 percent of the portfolio.

I'm concerned that things are looking like they will get worse in the market before they get better. It feels like every month we are getting closer to a recession.

I am frustrated by inflexible investment options:

My wealth manager only offers a limited range of investment products, and often I find they are not suitable for my investment goals.

I get frustrated when I'm not allowed to make changes to my investments.

I get very annoyed when I incur penalties and fees just for withdrawing funds.

My biggest fears, barriers and uncertainties are:

I use a tech platform for my investments and my funds get locked in, there are unforeseen huge fees, it makes bad speculative investments, it doesn't give me adequate updates about how my investments are tracking.

If the above resonates, then please know that you're in the right place and you are reading the right book.

Those fears, prejudices, uncertainties and beliefs are common across our clients when we meet them. Whether they decide to work with us or go it alone, we show them there are better ways. We show them there are solutions to all of these fears.

Ultimately, we shape their mindset into a winning mindset, we help eliminate the old faithful fears and frustrations bred into us by the marketplace, and most importantly, we help them to beat their market benchmark.

I am confident we can assist you to do exactly the same.

Let's read on.

WHY WEALTH MANAGERS UNDERPERFORM THEIR MARKET BENCHMARKS AND WHY THIS WILL NEVER CHANGE.

The wealth management model as we know it is not designed to help investors beat their market benchmark. Let me reiterate that point, it is *not* designed to help investors like you and I to beat the market.

Yet, it's bred into us as soon as we start earning money (or inheriting it) that in order to build wealth we need to build an investment portfolio and of course we have to work with a trusted wealth manager or IFA, or more often than not, the financial advisor used by your parents, and maybe even their parents before them.

Well, at least one part of that statement is right.

'In order to build wealth, we need to build an investment portfolio'.

However, I hope when you read this book, you'll quickly realise that many of the other half truths (at best) that surround this marketplace can be eliminated quickly.

I started this chapter by saying that the wealth management model isn't designed to help investors beat their market benchmark. Let me elaborate.

Using the traditional wealth management model makes it almost impossible for the everyday investor to beat the market. This statement derives from someone who has worked in this space on the coalface of the markets for over two decades.

The world of high finance and asset management is a large one, but it's full of analysts, advisors, back-office employees, middle office paper shufflers, business relationship managers, asset allocators, economists and salesmen.

Most of these individuals have never placed a trade in the markets in their lifetimes, and probably never will. Yet, they're still entrusted with our hard-earned wealth!

The world of traders within this world is made up of a very small portion of individuals. The world of successful market beating traders, well that is much much smaller.

This is the world that Ed and I grew up in, and have always resided in, and from afar we could most certainly conclude that there is a large problem in the wealth management space.

How can a large collection of some of the greatest minds globally fail to build funds and strategies that consistently outperform simple market trackers?

It just doesn't make sense.

Unless you accept, that the model was NEVER DESIGNED TO BEAT MARKET BENCHMARKS.

Before providing further thoughts on this, let me present some visual statistics as I hate to make bold statements like the above without evidence to back up the claims:

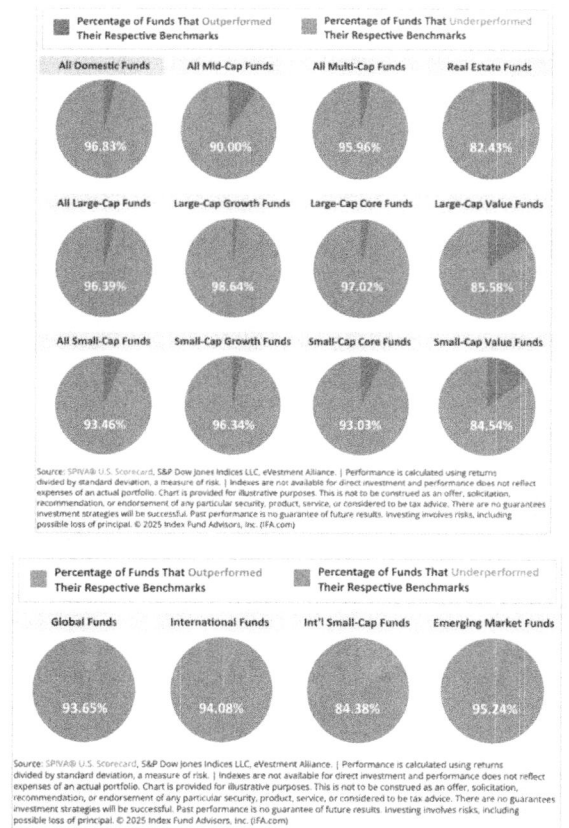

The above shows the percentage of funds that outperformed and underperformed their benchmark over the last 20 years. The underperformance slice of the pie is substantially larger.

Therefore, I think it would be generous for me to say that over 80% of fund managers and their active funds underperform simple market trackers. Very generous indeed..

Although many of these statistics are hard to stomach, it validates what I've been saying to anyone that will listen for the last decade:

If your money is tied into the traditional wealth management space, you will rarely beat your market benchmark, and it is *impossible* to do it consistently.

Let me explain why:

If your standard wealth manager takes your capital, and automatically diversifies some of your portfolio into bonds and cash, then instantly you're restricted on the upside in your investment portfolio structure.

Yes, diversification is a great tool, a much-needed tool, but do you really need to pay your advisor 1.5-2 percent to place YOUR money into a high interest account or government bond?

I imagine not.

Yet, even when interest rates were residing at rock bottom for many years, we still handed over our money to our advisor, and guess what they did with a portion of our capital?

Yes, you may have guessed it: They placed a portion of it into cash and bonds.

Now here is where it gets really ridiculous. At stages in the low-interest rate cycle, some governments (Germany included) were paying negative interest rates.

What do I mean by this?

I mean that you were *paying* them to hold your money. Yes, with negative interest rates, if you bought government bonds, you had to pay for the privilege of holding them.

However, guess what?

Advisors and asset allocators would still allocate your capital to them. Why? Because they don't know any different, they've never placed a trade in their lifetimes and they follow 'asset allocation templates' which diversify a portfolio, but generally ensure you'll never perform well, and very very rarely (unless you have a lucky allocation) will you beat your market benchmark.

Even in a normal interest rate climate, where you're not *paying* large governments to hold your capital, you might be receiving somewhere between 3-4 percent interest/bond yield on this portion of your capital.

Therefore, if the 'asset allocation professional' is following the standard 60/40 allocation model (stocks and bonds) your investment portfolio will already be struggling to keep pace with the general appreciation in the value of global stocks/equities.

Like I said earlier, holding a portion of your capital in cash and bonds is a great idea, but please don't pay your wealth manager 1.5-2 percent for the privilege. Any gain they might accrue for you will quickly be eliminated via the fees.

KEY TAKE AWAY: If you persist with your wealth manager allocating a large portion of your portfolio into cash and bonds, as it's a very passive strategy, ensure the fees reflect this. Also, ask which bonds they're investing into. Are they safe (AAA rated), are they offering a solid yield? Make them more accountable.

At this stage in the above investment journey, with the diversification (60/40 split) our wealth manager or IFA offers us, we're already trading and trending behind the curve when it comes to beating our market benchmark if we're comparing our overall portfolio performance against some of the global equity markets which many investors do.

Here are the long-term performances for global equities. These are the compounded returns on a per annum basis since the year 2000:

Index	Compound annual growth rate
CAC 40	5.89%
DAX	6.00%
Dow Jones Industrial Average	9.44%
EURO STOXX 50	4.16%
FTSE 100	5.01%
MSCI World	7.15%
S&P 500	8.95%

Therefore, if 40 percent of our portfolio is underperforming these markets after being allocated into cash or bonds, with the other 60 percent we're already playing catch up.

The best thing of all; I haven't even mentioned the fees charged by your asset manager yet.

I hope you're beginning to understand that within the traditional world of wealth management, not only is it hard to beat your market benchmark (even if that benchmark is a lower yielding FTSE 100), in fact it is probably impossible to do this over any length of time.

However, we hope to tilt the odds in your favour through this book.

I've been known to say that most wealth managers are actually holding your portfolio hostage. It's quite the claim but let me explain what I mean.

I'm referring to the exorbitant fees you're paying a wealth manager who is (almost certainly) generating you sub-par returns.

For years, nobody questioned the necessity of the fund manager. These superhuman stock pickers won "star" status for their semi-mythical ability to thrash the wider market, making grateful investors rich in the process.

Then the myth started to unravel, as research repeatedly showed that three quarters of fund managers actually underperformed the market.

Soon investors began to wake up to the fact that the only person making money was the manager themselves, through the lavish fees on their funds.

The truth is, instead of beating the market, the vast majority of managers are beaten by it.

What's fascinating is the sheer scale of long-term underperformance. Incredibly, the numbers show that fund managers are even worse than you probably think.

In 2022, during a time when stock pickers should have earned their money as markets fell and placing money in the right place was so important, it was actually the worst year for UK stock pickers in 20 years of data.

Fewer than 10 percent of funds outperformed their respective benchmarks. In 2023 when tech boomed on the back of AI: once again most managers lagged their benchmark.

S&P Global, a financial data firm, found that actively managed UK equity and UK large and mid-cap equity funds recorded underperformance rates of 92 percent and 97 percent in 2022 and 2023.

Returns in 2022 were driven by the oil and mining sectors, as commodity prices rose in the wake of Russia's invasion of Ukraine, as well as "defensive" pharmaceutical and consumer stocks.

However, many active fund managers missed out on these gains.

For US shares, 67 percent of active fund managers failed to beat their benchmark in 2022, while for European shares 83 percent failed to do so. Three-quarters of global funds and emerging market funds failed to outperform last year. In 2023 and 2024, once again, it was pretty similar.

For US stock funds, 98 percent fail to outperform over 10 years, and 94 percent after five years. Global funds are nearly as bad, with 93 percent failing to outperform over ten years and 89 percent failing to do so over five years, according to S&P.

S&P found that active fund managers did not perform better in down markets, despite what many fund managers argue.

It gets worse. Over ten years, 100 percent of active emerging markets equity funds failed to beat their benchmark, the S&P. That's right, every single one.

Despite this, fund managers continued to rake in millions of pounds in earnings, while investors like you and I were forced to bear the bulk of the losses.

Let me shed some light on the hidden costs of the current wealth management model.

Asset management companies claim that the very best fund managers can add value, and a handful might do, although rarely the same handful year after year. However, in the longer run the majority do not.

The picture is even worse when you consider that wealth managers charge a premium for underperformance, with initial fees of up to 5 percent of your money, and annual management charges ranging from 0.75 percent to 1.75 percent.

Many say the answer is therefore to invest in a tracker. Fair enough. They're cheap, and by their very definition, they can't underperform their benchmark.

Let's have a look at the long-term performance of a few indices again:

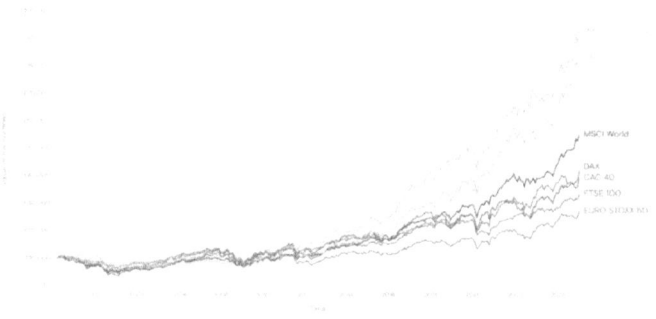

As you can see, just tracking these indices will probably result in you beating nearly every fund manager. However, there are methods you can utilise that can compound this performance and later in this book we will be revealing these trade secrets and frameworks in the hope that we can empower investors everywhere.

In short, it is crystal clear that by working with a traditional wealth manager, you will underperform a simple market tracker.

After their attempt at diversification, their management fees, their performance fees (and numerous other fees) you're fighting a battle you just can't win.

IT IS IMPOSSIBLE TO CONSISTENTLY BEAT YOUR MARKET BENCHMARK WHEN WORKING WITH A TRADITIONAL WEALTH OR ASSET MANAGER.

Why we are bred to believe that working with a traditional wealth manager is the only way to invest is because the institutions have brain washed us into thinking so.

Why wouldn't they want us to believe that?

As I said earlier, when you're a fund with 150 billion GBP under management charging me 1.5 percent of my money per year that come rain, wind or shine, you will take, why wouldn't you want me to believe it's the only way?

The wealth management model isn't built for investors like you and I.

It is built for the shareholders of the largest banks and funds in the world.

It works brilliantly for them, they don't want this dynamic to change, and they will do anything they can to protect this status quo.

However, this book has already demonstrated that there is a large amount of underperformance. We have illustrated why and moving forward, we'll be explaining how you can change how you invest and join the movement of investors who are breaking away from a stale and outdated wealth management model. The asset management industry is evolving, and very soon, you'll be at the forefront of the evolution.

Read on, as we're only just getting started.

KNOWING THE REQUIREMENTS NEEDED TO BEAT YOUR MARKET BENCHMARK CONSISTENTLY.

In the last chapter, it's safe to say I bashed what I would term as a stale, and outdated wealth management model, an industry that I believe is ripe for disruption.

However, as much as I do believe that it is impossible to consistently beat your market benchmark working with an 'old school' financial advisor or wealth manager, for *long term* growth of your portfolio, the model can work.

The key is working with a cost-efficient advisor (they are out there somewhere), and allocating your portfolio to them at the right time.

If the FTSE 100 retraces 10 percent from highs; BUY. If US tech drops 10-15 percent from their highs; BUY.

Allocate your capital, hold for the long term, keep the costs low and reap the rewards.

If you ever have a further tranche of capital you're looking to invest, do exactly the same. Rinse and repeat.

Be patient, wait for an opportunity; and then allocate.

Will you consistently BEAT YOUR MARKET BENCHMARK? Possibly. However, if you don't, you'll be extremely close. Depending of course on what your benchmark is.

The model can work, but you need to know who to work with, and how to play the game.

Let me be brutally succinct here. As an investor your number one priority should be **to build a portfolio that is as close to a general market performance as possible** (or even better; to beat it).

Do not be satisfied with underperforming the markets by 3-4 percent each and every year. 3-4 percent might not sound like a lot to you (it does to me), but over the years, by not compounding the extra 3-4 percent per annum, you are leaving a lot of wealth on the table.

Building a portfolio structure like this is not something you do on the side, or something you completely outsource or delegate. Without being dramatic, it's probably the most important variable you can tweak that will impact the wealth of your family for potentially generations to come.

It doesn't matter how successful you are in your career, if you aren't building an effective investment portfolio structure your entire existence as an investor is pointless.

If you have a portfolio that can consistently beat the markets (or match them as a worse case), your results over the longer term can be phenomenal.

If you don't, then your wealth curve can become unpredictable, unreliable and ultimately, stressful. This is because the future of your lifestyle, your wealth and your family, even for generations to come, will be impacted by your poor portfolio structure.

Feel free to ignore this fact and pretend that everything is fine as it is. Alternatively: Devour this book and make the required changes and modifications. Do not become one of the depressing statistics in the marketplace.

Whatever you decide to do, please know that the answer isn't some shiny new trading strategy, or some 'algo' that generates 'guaranteed returns'. They're all gimmicks.

Accumulating more strategies/tip sheets/or expert advice aren't the solutions, and deep down, I think you probably know this. Because if you're like most investors, you've gone through all of these wealth managers, you've subscribed to all of the financial news channels, received the tip sheets, even tried trading and investing for yourself, only to find minimal improvement.

The reason for this is because they're all trying to find that holy grail, something that might not be possible.

They're not curing the systematic problems with the wealth management model. I hope this book can do this for you.

The answer is in understanding how the model works and then making some subtle tweaks and modifications to your portfolio that takes it from a portfolio that tracks the markets, into one that beats your market benchmark consistently. It really is as simple as that.

HERE WE GO:

In this book, I am going to inform you of things that most people in the industry either don't know or would not tell you for fear of losing their jobs. The methods in this book could even be viewed as controversial.

Not because they're untrue, but because they're more factual than anything else you've ever been taught about investing.

What you will discover in this book will likely change everything for you. The way you think, the way you look at the world of finance, and how much money you make each year.

You see, after working with thousands of investors over the years, I've realised that before they meet me, they all follow pretty much the same approach. It might be with a different financial advisor or wealth manager, but still, it's the same (or a very similar) approach.

Most investors believe that there is only one way to invest, and they follow that approach. They are the expert in their chosen domain, so they work with the 'expert' in the asset management field, and I understand why they would.

However, what they don't realise is that the cards are stacked against them. The probability of outperforming the markets is minimal.

Every year they hear the same excuses. 'It was a tough year out there', 'We got caught up in the sell off', 'The FTSE has been lagging its peers', 'US tech is just too volatile to have too much exposure in' and on and on they go.

'But it will be different next year'.

It never is, and then five-ten years down the line, they try the next asset manager or advisor their business partner or brother-in-law has told them about.

The cycle repeats.

Until it finally reaches a stage where there is even a level of acceptance that 'this is how it is'.

Trust me, it doesn't have to be like that.

It doesn't matter what level of expertise your advisor claims to have, whether they've been an IFA for 3 decades, supported your parents, or grown their business by 500 percent; all that matters is *your portfolio performance*. However, with a system rigged against you, the rest is irrelevant.

To be a successful investor, you *must* take control of the direction of your portfolio. It is impossible to beat the market if you do not.

The only way to do this is to invest more of your time, attention and energy into the number one thing that will build your wealth, building a portfolio structure that can beat your market benchmark.

The time, and effort diverted towards this could change your life forever.

I have seen these portfolio modifications implemented across the world. Whoever they are, whatever their experience, it works.

Because if your portfolio consistently beats markets and your wealth compounds far quicker than you could have ever imagined, life becomes a very different place.

Building a better portfolio structure isn't a choice; it is an obligation. Don't be complacent and do what your father did. Make a change and evolve before the wealth management model does. Change is coming, the only question is, when will you embrace it?

In these coming chapters, I will show you how to become a master at building a portfolio structure that will outperform your market benchmark and leave your wealth manager a country mile behind in performance terms.

Everything you are about to learn is easy to implement, and I'll teach you the lessons my business partner and I learnt from over 4 decades in total of trading in an ever-changing marketplace.

However, before I get ahead of myself.

Why the hell should you listen to a word I say? Who is Lane Clark and what is this company, TPP, that he has built with his business partner?

Fair questions. Let me provide you with the answers.

Let me preface the answer by stating that the nuggets of wisdom and market expertise provided in this book haven't derived from me sitting around analysing markets, reading books, and offering my guidance based on this theory.

No way.

It's based on over two decades in the mix, up against the coalface, and on the front line of trading and investing. I've collected the battle wounds on my search to find the solutions.

If there was a trading philosophy that piqued my interest I found it, I tested it, I tweaked it. If there was a market guru who had consistently outperformed, I immersed myself in what they'd done, how they'd done it, and refined versions of this for myself to test in the marketplace.

If there was an arbitrage situation that traders were taking advantage of for themselves or the fund they worked for, I would be exploring it for myself.

In my years as a trader and investor, I have spoken with some of the greats, watched every video, read every book from the best traders in history to find out if there was anything I could add to my own methodology.

However, I was never completely satisfied with what I found (despite some great guidance) because the truth was:

A large proportion of what I heard was based on bygone climates. Markets where it was harder to lose money than make money. I say that with the greatest respect, but the global climate we reside in now is different.

Therefore, in the end, I always took the wisdom but interpreted it in ways that work in the market today. Not yesterday, not last year, but today, and every day moving forward.

When I say 'every' day, I don't mean I expect to be positive in every trading day. I'm not a magician or miracle worker. What I do mean is that I expect the strategies and structures that work for me now will work forever. Month in and month out. Quarter in and quarter out, and when the bad runs come (they do) I know that by sticking with a methodology that consistently works, that in the end, they will deliver.

I see myself (equally the rest of our traders on TPP) as an excellent trader, and with my proven process and methodology even the best fund managers out there if placed head to head, may struggle to compete. Anyway, let me explain where it all started……

WORKING CLASS AND VERY AWARE OF THE NEED FOR HARD WORK.

I grew up in a small town in Northamptonshire called Corby. Some termed it as 'mini Scotland' as the population increased massively when an influx of Scottish folk moved into the town for the steelworks (my parents' generation). It is a very working-class environment, but a place I have very fond memories of, and have lots of friends I'm still very close with.

People work hard for what little they have, and often with a smile on their faces.

My sister and I were brought up by our parents, who never let us go short despite having very little money to spare.

My mum sometimes worked multiple jobs to keep food on the table, as my Dad realised the steelworks weren't for him and went back to school in his 30's.

Times were probably tough for them, but they never let it impact us. It didn't matter that in one of our houses we didn't have a carpet in it for years, or when the same house was repossessed one day when my sister and I returned home from school. We just moved onto the next chapter. I can still remember young, cheeky (and chubby) me wondering what the hell was going on, but looking back, it is something I can smile about now.

When we became old enough to work, we'd fit our studies around working whenever time would allow. I'd work in factories for weeks and months on end, working whatever hours they would offer me whenever I had a holiday from school.

Working in minus 25-degree freezers or loading 25KG bags onto the back of a lorry for 12 hours a day, every day isn't fun, but it definitely instils character into you, and if anything, it made me realise that I wanted more for myself than that.

Why on earth am I telling you all of this in a book about 'beating the markets'?

Because I learnt at an early age that nothing in life comes without hard work, nothing is given to you. You don't always get what you deserve, and you have to scratch, claw and fight to get where you want to be in life.

This work ethic has served me well in my life. I didn't have the fortunate up bringing of some, but I have loved every minute (well most of it), have very little regrets, and it has made me who I am today.

These valuable lessons learnt early have served me successfully throughout my life.

When I finished Uni, I took this work ethic to the city. I was 22, baby faced, and ready to 'take over' The City. I'll never forget how it started.

My sister informed me about a role an up-and-coming brokerage were looking to fill where they were looking for 'young, ambitious, driven graduates'. Great, I ticked the boxes, but would they really want a young lad from Corby when they could have recruited grads from some of the best schools and Uni's in the country?

It was a group interview on the trading floor and there were about 25 young hungry grads who were invited along. I got the role alongside 3 others from the Evening.

The journey was underway.

I'd love to say the next day I was learning how to trade, but the reality is, I was 'cold calling' 300 prospects a day and offering them a brochure and a call with a 'senior broker'. Luckily, this work ethic of mine came to the fore, and I made an impression quite quickly with some of my seniors.

These principles serve me to this day. I rise early every day, I have a plan I will execute every day, and goals to hit every day. Those goals might not be to make 300-400 cold calls, but I am always willing to work to achieve my goals.

Why I'm saying this is because whoever you are, whatever you do, whatever background you are from, if you instil this ethic (or one similar) into what you're doing, you will become more successful.

I could give you the tactics and techniques required, but if you're not prepared to implement them, you're probably best putting this book down now.

Controlling the controllables and having a strong work ethic is something that alongside the right approach, will help you beat your market benchmark.

Be relentless in your work ethic and desire to beat markets. No gimmicks, no 'get rich quick schemes', no fancy new shiny wealth manager. Don't wait for this to happen to you and your portfolio. Make it happen.

I'm not here to say changing how you have always invested and what you have always believed is easy. Most people like to sugarcoat things, and just talk about the results, the outcomes, or post their success online.

You won't get that with me. You'll get brutal honesty alongside the insight. In this book I'll tell you how you can beat your market benchmark. However, I can take the horse to the water, but I can't make you drink it.

Beating market benchmarks isn't for everyone. You need the approach, the techniques and the mindset.

Feed a man a fish and he'll eat for a day, teach a man to fish and he'll eat for life. In this book, I'll provide you with the tools to fish in the markets and beat them in your lifetime.

You must be completely zoned in on succeeding. No excuses are allowed. Be accountable, take responsibility for every bit of success and failure that comes your way. Own it.

Kill the voice inside, make the right decisions, stay the course, reap the rewards.

If you're serious about succeeding, know that it's a commitment for life. There is no time off from building a world class portfolio structure. Don't get me wrong, it's not a full-time job (you already have that) but don't ever get complacent and fall back into those bad habits.

If you follow the approach and principles laid out in this book, you **will** be successful. I will give you the tools required, but it will take work and monitoring.

If you're ready, if you're hungry, if you think this is for you, then let's get this show on the road.

THE MULTI-MILLION-POUND LEARNING CURVE. (YES, THERE HAVE BEEN SOME PAINFUL LESSONS WHICH YOU CAN LEARN FROM).

Before writing this book, I took a trip down memory lane, and I tried to remember every technique I had ever tried in the world of trading/investing from the very early days of my career.

It would be great to think that someone who is a self-taught trader could have had a plain sailing path to success but it's safe to say I haven't.

In fact, I keep an extensive trade log going back decades and mistakes I've made and events I've been exposed to previously have lost millions of GBP's. Yes, millions!

Now don't get me wrong (and please don't start crying for me) I've made substantially more than the hard lessons have cost me along the way, but by learning from my expensive lessons, you can build a portfolio that performs without the need for the expensive errors, and the painful lessons.

Any trader you will ever meet will have had some form of 'expensive lesson' and I'm no different.

However, I am a 100 percent advocate, that 'you win or you learn', and anytime a trade has gone against me, or an unexpected event has happened, I will take responsibility, ask myself if there is anything I would have done differently (with the power of hindsight) and if there are lessons to be learned, tweaks to be made, then I will learn those lessons and make those tweaks.

The thing is, looking back I realise that most of my lessons were because I was chasing returns that probably weren't possible. The trade that looked too good to be true (they generally are), the position that was destined to make me a fortune, but because I took on excessive leverage, I couldn't hold the trade. The 'short sell' position against a raging bull market. The trades that were stopped out regularly because my stop losses were too tight. The pegged currency that was one day unpegged, the high dividend stock that became worthless overnight, the FX pair that trended in the opposite direction for over one year. The IFA with the track record of beating his benchmark consistently until he took me on as a client. The illiquid stock I couldn't get out of. Yep, it's safe to say there have been many many lessons along the way.

There is no holy grail, there is no way to make 500 percent in one year, the market doesn't owe you anything.

Some of those trade errors possibly resonate with you, most of them are done EVERY day in the market. I want to ensure you avoid them.

The market is a great humbler, and as soon as you begin to think you've cracked it, an event unfolds that nobody was expecting.

Take on too much risk, and it could be the end of your investment journey.

Even to this day, I am aware enough to realise that there will be other 'black swan' events I wasn't expecting, but although they're always painful, I understand they're par for the course. I'll manage risk in the volatile moments, and if I am being candid, I will probably end up making money from the event.

I want you to have the ability and the acumen to do exactly the same.

It was after making the mistakes that I made, being exposed to the events that I have, that I realised that as good as I thought I was, I could always be better.

I went back and studied all of the greats. I looked at their expensive errors as well.

Have a look for yourself, it isn't hard to find.

Rat Dalio is one of the world's greatest investors. However, it wasn't always like this:

> Ray founded Bridgewater Associates in 1975 not as a hedge fund, but as an advisory firm. He offered consulting services on how to navigate the financial landscape and published a paid newsletter read by big clients like McDonalds and Nabisco.
>
> After seven years, Ray had built a team and a solid client base, but success started to go to his head: "I couldn't have been more arrogant at that time" he said.
>
> Ray was also trading markets personally, making accurate predictions and building a cash pile. Confidence was sky high, so he decided to go 'all in' on a significant personal trade that bet on a global economic downturn.
>
> However, the exact opposite happened...
>
> Markets started an incredible bull run and Ray was wiped out.
>
> "I was left with nothing—no money, no people. I was so broke I had to borrow $4,000 from my Dad" he recalled.
>
> At only 33-years-old, his reputation was in tatters.

This story above isn't unique. We have all done it.

However, I will help you to avoid it....

Look into some of these legends, learn from their errors, or take my words of advice that I have studied their mistakes, made many of my own, but built a formula that consistently beats my market benchmark.

Like I said; 'You win, or you learn'.

As well as their errors, I also studied their psychology. Human psychology is a crazy thing, and it can also be a wrecker of investment philosophies.

It's hard to hold a trade if it goes against you day after day, week after week, but if you believe in it, if you are sticking with your methodology, then you have to hold.

If the dynamics behind the trade change, if you then need to get out, don't be afraid to cut that loss. Don't let pride get in the way of profit.

As an investor or a trader, you need to accept you'll be wrong. It is impossible to be right every time. However, if you can build a methodology where you are right more than you're wrong, and have winners that are larger than your losers, then you'll have a winning approach.

I aim to show you exactly how to do this.

At this point, you may be thinking why would Lane share all of this knowledge, experience, learnings from expensive errors to me for such a low price point? To be candid, it's a fair question to ask.

However, in my mind; it's simple.

Success in any walk of life is hard. Anybody who says it is easy isn't telling you the truth. Success (e.g. beating the markets) in a world and industry where the odds are stacked against you, is even harder.

However, for the few who manage to do so (like the verified trading track records on TPP), doors have probably been opened on the way, knowledge given, experience passed on, which has helped an eager learner and hard worker like me to develop a winning approach. I see it as my duty to send the elevator back down. Good people do good things. Happy karma.

From where I am sitting right now, we've made multiple millions of GBP's for clients globally of all shapes and sizes through my career, and since facilitating TPP our average strategy has been making around 20 percent per annum since inception. Like I said, it is definitely possible to beat your market benchmark, and using the tactics we've designed, we're starting a movement that is changing how many investors invest. Over the next decade or two, the world of wealth management will change and evolve, solutions to the underperforming overpaid model will be sought, but our techniques and our company are ahead of this curve.

After reading this book, I hope you will be ahead of the pack as well.

Along the way, we've learnt a lot, and every day we aim to learn more. We will continue to offer our learnings on our journey. Of that, you have my word.

It's this deep understanding of the investment world and being aware of the pitfalls that has allowed TPP to thrive.

Since we formed, we've been called 'The Future of Investing' on the London Stock Exchange website. Shares magazine said, 'We might be the solution for frustrated investors', and Market Watch said 'TPP are changing investing for investors globally'.

I've been asked to speak on stages around the world and featured on the same events on the same days as market legends like Ray Dalio and Jamie Dimon.

Our business also broke records when we embarked on our first fund raise.

Have you heard of the challenger bank Monzo?

When they started on their journey to disrupt a stale and outdated (sound familiar?) traditional banking world, they raised 1m GBP in 96 seconds when their fund-raising campaign was launched.

They actually have a meeting room called 'The World Record Room' in their head office.

I have always believed that if you build something disruptive, something that empowers people, and makes things better for them, that people will back it.

Monzo proved that.

However, their 96 second 1m GBP raise was obliterated by our 36 second 1m GBP fund raiser for our business.

Again, if you build something to help people, the masses will back it.

I hope this book will start to help you to beat your market benchmark. I hope it will assist you to become substantially wealthier.

My point with most of the above is, I like to think I know what I'm talking about, and I am going to share with you the results of decades worth of trial and error, testing, tweaking, money made, money lost, mistakes, learnings etc. You're not going to learn the flavour of the month this month, a strategy that is here today, but gone tomorrow. You're going to learn an approach to the market that has worked for 1000's of people and going way beyond mine and Ed's decades of experience in the marketplace.

Long term strategies that you can build your portfolio and wealth on.

Sadly, in today's 'get rich quick' world where instant results and satisfaction are required, we're inundated with the next great trading tools and advice.

Go on social media and you'll quickly find:

How to learn how to trade in 3 weeks.

What cryptos to buy with upside potential of 1000 percent.

How to use options for a low-risk high return strategy.

Buy these US tech stocks now to find the next Nvidia or Apple.

The technical trading systems that get 90 percent of trades right.

Ladies/Gents, as great as the theory behind the above sounds great. The reality is very very different. Here is the hard-hitting truth; None of the above really matters.

You can have all the shiny new toys and techniques, but unless you have the right mindset, approach, and techniques, you'll never beat the market.

In fact, you'd probably be better off leaving your capital with your stale and outdated financial advisor.

In contrast, what I hope this book and learnings will provide to you, is a methodology that you can adopt, ingrain into your portfolio structure, and beat your market benchmark with for years to come.

In the following pages, I will teach you to do all of this and more. These techniques have been tailored to work in today's ruthlessly competitive world of investing and have proven to work for nearly every investor regardless of wealth and experience level.

INVESTING ABILITY MULTIPLIED: THE ONLY SKILL YOU'LL NEED TO BUILD A WINNING PORTFOLIO:

If we go back in time to when I got my start in The City, I was far removed from actually investing into the markets.

I talk about the financial advisors who have never placed a trade in the markets in their career, yet at the start, I was just the same.

Relentlessly cold calling prospects and letting them know about our company and our services was all I did.

I remember wondering back then why people were so resistant to hearing about what I had to tell them about our company and the services we provided. The penny finally dropped.

They didn't care about me, our company, nor our great US stock ideas, they only cared about themselves, and *their* investment returns!

Quickly my sales presentations evolved from talking about our company, our products, our USP's, and anything else about our company, to talking about how we could benefit **'them'**.

That was all clients cared about, and by knowing that early in my journey, and combining that with my relentless work ethic, I knew if I aligned with a company (or built my own company) where we could build products that helped *them* to beat the market and charged *them* less than our competitors did, then we really would be onto something. We could change the game.

It was almost like I had 'cracked the code' of what the market needed, but I was probably too young and inexperienced to build the product or company the people needed.

However, time was on my side.

FURTHER DEVELOPMENT:

Skipping forward a couple of years, I realised that whilst working in the 'sales side' of finance helped me understand what clients wanted, I needed to find a way to deliver it for them. I had moved onto the 'trading side' of the business. It was time to build the strategies and techniques my earlier experience of conversing with investors taught me that they needed and more importantly, wanted.

With everything I had read, everyone I had studied, and all the techniques I had explored, I knew destiny was calling.

However, it was far from easy.

I started working with the retail brokers in the UK, but never understood why my trades were often stopped out overnight, or why my stop loss order was often nudged before the markets bounced back.

At this stage I didn't realise they increased their bid/ask spreads at night to capture the amateur traders' stop-loss.

Lessons were learned quickly.

Was this why no one ever traded themselves? It was a lot harder than I imagined. Was this why the FCA make brokers state how many people lose money when working with them, and most even now have statistics of over 70 percent of losing investors?

In my opinion, these results are almost unbelievable.

Perhaps the techniques were solid, but the brokers I was aligning with weren't.

I took my business elsewhere. To brokers I could trust. Institutional brokers.

I traded like a macro trader, a technical trader. I studied charts, read reports, built position sizing models, and back tested hundreds of strategies repeatedly.

I began to think my 'timing of trades' was excellent.

My technical trading expertise was starting to pay off.

All these years of trading, the mistakes made, the lessons learnt, I was getting there.

Had I found the 'trading holy grail'?

I was still only very young, but it was time to set up my own Asset Manager. After all, I had built one from 3 employees to a 40 strong team for someone else and built their AUM (assets under management) almost from scratch.

I was ready. I was hungry like nobody else, I had traded for years in many different styles, and I had refined a winning technique.

Off I went, and I recruited those closest to me. The dream team was in place.

For a number of years, things were great. We were providing clients with exactly what they wanted. They were fed up with the 4-5 percent they were getting from the traditional wealth management model, they wanted more. My team and I were delivering for them.

Word was spreading quickly, and the funds were flooding in. Brokers wanted to align and allocate their client money as well (yes, even those pesky retail brokers!). The revolution was underway.

We were ready to change how the world invested. We had learnt so much over the years and as a team were growing up together like brothers. World domination beckoned. Life could not have been any better.

But then, out of nowhere a number of expensive lessons in the space of one minute in one day….

Lessons that would be painful, life changing, humbling, and one's that finally set me on the path to build an approach that beats the markets regardless of the market climate.

I will never get ahead of myself and think that I can't learn any more than I have done already. In fact, every day I am always looking to learn more. I work 14-15 hours a day, I listen to audio books in my spare time, I am a voracious reader, I absorb information like a sponge, I have a thirst for knowledge.

However, I expect that the lessons moving forward remain small one's which on the back of, I can make small tweaks and improvements to build a more robust model.

January the 15th 2015 was far, far more than this.

Now I know we're talking more than a decade ago, and I know I've become far wiser in this period, but I still remember this day like it was yesterday.

Every trader has their 'big negative event' and this was mine.

I didn't see it coming. I was beginning to feel invincible, but without it, I wouldn't be who I am today.

Life's experiences shape us.

Back to the event:

It was roughly 9.15am, I was sipping on my third latte of the day, and after our morning trading meeting, we were plotting for the day ahead.

What options were out there for us today? Where could we snare a profit from?

Equities? FX? Commodities?

Wherever the opportunity was, we would find it.

But then, we noticed on one of our screens that one of our trading accounts' equity levels was highlighted pink. Pink? Doesn't that mean a margin call?

At first, we felt it must have been a glitch, but then there was multiple.

In fact, at the time it felt like it was pink everywhere we looked.

WTF....

We checked our Bloombergs to catch the headline within milliseconds of the movement, but couldn't work out what it was?

We searched online, we tried to call the broker, we called contacts in the industry. Panic was setting in.

And then the headline hit the screens.

The Swiss National Bank (The SNB) which had pegged their currency to the Euro at a floor of 1.20 had removed the peg.

The 'fail safe' trade that had provided 'free money' for us for months on end, had just imploded.

Only one week before the event, the SNB had reassured the market that despite market forces they remained committed to the peg.

They had our back....

WTF.

How could they do this to us? Our clients?

The Swiss Franc which had been trading in a range between 1.20 (the floor) and 1.24 (the profit zone) all of a sudden was trading at 0.80 v's the Euro.

A movement of over 30 percent in a split second, in a market where many were leveraged. Some as high as 100 x's!

However, amidst the panic, it clicked for Sammy (who worked with us):

"Lane don't panic, because we always wait until the trade moves close to the floor before buying, we have stop loss orders in place just under our entry, and looking at the market movement, although incredibly sharp the brokers should have been able to exit," he said in his reassuring voice.

"What about the margin calls on the screen? That can't be right, can it?" I asked in response.

'I expect that'll be their software not operating correctly due to the extreme movements, but let's check- I'm pretty sure the trades will be closed out' Sammy reassured the team.

A collective sigh of relief went around the office.

Let's call the broker.

Now without throwing anyone under the bus, the broker was Alpari UK Ltd. At the time, a fast-growing brokerage that sponsored the West Ham football team. Yes, they were one of those pesky retail brokers, but we had a great relationship with them.

Things will be ok, but lessons will still be learnt.

We called their office…..

Nothing…….

We called again….

Nothing…..

Someone chipped in- 'Lads, relax- they'll be fending calls galore at the moment if their trading software is failing. Give them 5 minutes'.

We rang again….

Nothing…

Again…

Nothing..

At the same time, it still looked like margin calls galore on our portfolios…

However, they hadn't closed the trades (on the trading software). This had to mean they'd been closed in reality, but we just couldn't see it yet….

We hoped…

We called again…

Nothing…

As we only worked one skyscraper away from them, one of the team suggested that they'd go and visit them.

'Sorry, no one is available to meet you today' was the message reported back to Matt when he visited.

This was strange.

Finally, we decided we'd be better having a strategy meeting to discuss all of the different permutations.

So many thoughts were spinning around our heads; What if Alpari doesn't answer, what if the trades are still open, what if they closed them in massive losses, what do we tell the clients, do we tell them now, send a group message out, contact everyone individually.

So many moving parts, but one thing was for sure, there would be some lessons learnt on the back of this once the dust settles.

Late in the Evening, and still no sign of our 'retail broker' and then the news broke.

Alpari UK Ltd have gone into administration.

Wow, if there were unanswered questions before, there were even more now!

Fast forward about 6 hours into the early morning, and an email had dropped through from KPMG (the administrator) chasing losses on client accounts.

What about our stops? Did the stops fail? What about the trading software? Did the trades even close?

Like I said, lessons would be learned….

Cutting a long story short, this situation got so messy that I ended up paying hundreds of thousands of GBPs to one of the City's best law firms to fight for our clients, and to try and recover their losses that we felt were caused on the back of Alpari's failings.

We won (as in they stopped chasing us for the excess losses), but it didn't feel like that.

Lost revenue, lost client capital, badly bruised egos, our custodian who held our clients' funds no longer around, our own business was in disarray!

Wow, and to think before the events of Jan the 15th 2015, for a number of years we thought we had it cracked.

We were of the opinion that there were no lessons that needed learning. We thought we had the holy grail.

How wrong we were!

Like I said earlier, the experiences in our lifetimes shape who we are today, and perhaps the final lessons required were all dished out on a cold crisp morning in January 2015!

Stay away from retail brokers (yes, I had learnt this one again).

Never trade a 'pegged instrument' that can be manipulated by far larger forces than us.

There is no such thing as a 'too good to be true' trade.

Don't take on too much leverage. Black swan events can (and do) happen.

We already had some brilliant trading techniques, we were already regularly beating market benchmarks, we were making a difference, our timing of the markets was excellent, our methodology refined over a number of years, but maybe those final lessons were designed to happen all at the same time, to ensure that if we were going to make a difference in the investment world, we needed to know ALL of the pitfalls.

It was painful, but it was a game changer, and a decade later, I can see that it made me a better *investor*.

Yes, investor. I no longer saw myself as a trader as it felt too 'short term' and left me at the mercy of unexpected market events.

I had evolved into someone who had the exact same skillset as before, but who looked slightly longer term.

Yes, maybe some years you can make 150 percent on your portfolio, but if you take on that level of risk, and chase performance then at some stage something somewhere will go wrong.

I have been in this industry for over two decades, and I am telling you right now, despite having a spell of five-six years of regularly beating markets trading actively, before the CHF unpegging, I am yet to meet someone who has had a full career from being a successful day trader.

You'll hear the stories of the good months, the good quarters, the good years, or even an extended period like we had, but trade too actively and take on too much risk, and at some stage, something will go badly wrong.

With the volume I traded back in the day, retail brokers must have made a fortune. No wonder they liked me so much!

It's how many of them make their money. Volume, volume, volume.

On the back of these experiences (positive and negative), I was evolving as a trader (looking at the markets like an investor). I was also evolving as a person and as the years passed by, I began to assist other asset managers to design systems and strategies to beat the markets.

However, I knew I needed more, I knew if I really wanted to make the impact in the market that I intended, I needed to have my own investment vehicle again.

Enter my current (and probably my forever) business partner Edward Davies.

When we met (at the School Dads 5-a-side league), I realised we were very different. I was great at football (Ed had 2 left feet!). I am from a working-class background, Ed definitely wasn't. I was slightly on the loud side, Ed was quite reserved, I was outwardly very confident, Ed was internally assured of himself, and as I got to know him better, I thought, what a guy!

Intelligent, kind, honest, genuine, knowledgeable, thoughtful, a great family man, and best of all we shared similar trading backgrounds and we both had a vision to create something truly special and attempt to change how people invested.

We were both 'market beating' traders, but Ed was far more cautious, and despite evolving over the years myself, it was probably the influence of Ed that really brought me around to approaching the markets like I do these days.

He was the perfect person to meet at an opportune moment in my life.

I can't speak highly enough of Ed, how I've changed since I met him, and what we've built together, and although Ed will have had his share of 'expensive lessons' in the markets (like any trader who has been in the market long enough), it is with this combined knowledge and experience that we have managed to build what we've built now. It really is a special vehicle in my eyes, and it makes both of us proud.

A platform that showcases a variation of market beating trading strategies, which regardless of market climate, should keep you safe and should assist you to beat your benchmark year in and year out.

After reading this book, I hope I can assist you to beat your own benchmark.

2015 created a quantum shift in my mindset, and even though I had a skillset that already beat the markets consistently, the completely different approach to the markets (longer term time horizon) created a totally different and powerful dynamic to my investing/trading abilities.

The ability to beat your market benchmark consistently is by far the most lethal money-making skill you could ever hope to acquire.

I hope the lessons I have learned along the way, and the skillset I have built, will dramatically reduce your learning curve.

If you master these skills, you should never again have to worry about your portfolio growing, and your wealth expanding.

The bottom line is this, whatever industry you're in, whatever your experience, if you master the ability to beat markets consistently, life will have far less worries and frustrations.

You can make money with a long-term growth model in the markets, providing you dispense with the IFA or drive the costs down, and if you enter at the right time, but if you really want to beat your market benchmark consistently you need more.

To truly grow your wealth, you need an approach to markets that delivers come rain, wind or shine.

Listen carefully; in your own business/employment, you can hire people to deliver work for you, to train people, to set up technology, do your accounts. However, to get ahead in the financial markets, you need to take the responsibility yourself, and why wouldn't you if it's the most important metric you can change and tweak, which can make a material impact to your wealth now, and for generations to come.

I hope when you have read and digested the learnings in this book, that you can join the army of investors who are beginning to leave their wealth managers behind and have started to beat their market benchmarks.

SETTING YOUR STALL. REFINING YOUR APPROACH.

Before we dive incredibly deeply into the finer points of your new approach, it is worth reiterating some key details:

Right now, your portfolio probably underperforms a simple market tracker each year.

Why do I know that? Because over 80 percent of established and experienced active funds are in the same state.

You're overpaying for underperformance.

You're frustrated with the never-ending excuses from your wealth manager.

I might even go as far as saying that 'you feel stuck and out of options.' You're wondering if it is even possible to beat your market benchmark.

Maybe you've tried switching wealth managers, perhaps to someone cheaper. You may have even attempted to use a DIY investment platform. You've probably found out it's a lot cheaper but haven't had the time or perhaps the knowledge to improve your portfolio performance on your own.

Upon getting more frustrated, you may have even gone full circle and back to what you've always done.

Trust me, as I said previously, it doesn't have to be like this.

As we're moving into the key chapters, let me explain what you're going to learn once you read this book and implement the lessons.

You're going to learn:

How to build a portfolio that aims to beat your market benchmark consistently.

How to utilise three techniques that deliver year after year.

How to mitigate risk.

More importantly, I hope you'll be able to do this:

Without the need for your wealth manager or IFA.

Without paying any management or performance fees.

Without having to listen to the complicated jargon from your wealth manager and putting up with the lack of transparency on offer.

If you've progressed this far in the book, even despite everything I've said, you might still have these common concerns/misconceptions:

There aren't any options in the marketplace that consistently beat markets.

Everyone has a good pitch/story, but no approach is truly unique.

You don't think there are better options available than the 'old school' model you currently adopt with your investments.

If you still have these concerns, I will show you in the coming chapters how wrong you are.

Over recent years, we've changed the game for ourselves, and now we're doing likewise for frustrated investors just like you.

Clients and advocates of these strategies are now consistently beating their market benchmark each and every year, and in some cases by more than 1.5x.

These same methods work for investors with all levels of experience or knowledge levels. We've been told our approach has minimised market stress, and provided a low cost, market beating return.

Are you ready to change how you invest? Are you ready to make the required modifications to your portfolio structure?

Bryan Doyle was. He was frustrated with working with the UK's largest IFA/wealth manager (no names mentioned). He was of the opinion that they charged way too much, they locked him into the relationship (5-year lock in fee), and they also charged him for each and every fund they invested into (and they were all their own funds). Since working with our strategies Bryan has been liberated.

'Since working with these strategies my returns have been substantially more than my traditional portfolio performance. In fact, at times they've made 2 x market performance.'

However, before going any further:

Let me reiterate and stress once again who the lessons in this book are *not* for:

Investors looking for a 'get rich quick' trading program.

Investors with unrealistic expectations of growth (e.g. 50-100 percent per annum).

First time investors.

Investors who aren't open minded.

Investors who aren't fully committed to making the change required.

Now I've got that off my chest, let me tell you that based on my experience, this is who this revised approach to the markets is for:

Frustrated investors who are looking to modify their approach and finally *beat* their market benchmark.

Investors who are disillusioned with the stale and outdated wealth management model.

Investors who believe they overpay for underperformance.

Investors who have looked for alternative solutions but have yet to find one (hint; there aren't many).

Investors who have tried to take control of their own investments.

Over the coming chapters we're going to cover the following:

Part 1- Find out the big lie that your wealth manager has been selling you and why lining his or her pockets is crippling your investments. We will show you what you should be doing instead.

Part 2- Why passive strategies don't work as well as they should, and how you can modify this approach.

Part 3 (Chapters 10, 11 and 12)- The three insider tactics many successful investors and traders use to rarely lose and why they aren't common knowledge.

As you may sense, we're about to pick up the pace. Let's go.

THE BIG LIE THAT YOUR WEALTH MANAGER HAS BEEN SELLING YOU AND WHY LINING HIS OR HER POCKETS IS CRIPPLING YOUR INVESTMENTS.

Let's start with **the big lie**.

The wealth management model is not designed for investors to beat their market benchmark.

Why does nobody ever tell us this? I touched on it earlier but let me elaborate. Let me explain.

When you invest with your wealth manager, the typical model divides your capital following the 60/40 allocation model.

In very simple terms, this means they split your capital with 60 percent linked to stocks, and 40 percent linked to bonds/cash accounts.

Now please consider that although they will justify this as 'diversification' the reality is, the 40 percent that is allocated to bonds and cash will achieve less than your stock exposure every year.

Therefore, without looking at any other variables, with only 60 percent of your portfolio linked to the stock markets, how on earth can your overall portfolio beat a market tracker?

In fact, how can it even keep up with market returns?

Even if you had the FTSE 100 as your benchmark performance guide for your overall portfolio, the bonds and cash in your portfolio most years would generate less than that of the FTSE 100.

Look at this logically, if the average global stock market increases in value by 7 percent per annum, then if you had 100 percent of your portfolio spread across global markets without the fees, then you might just about be keeping up.

However, if your overpaid IFA is following his 'allocation model' that is dictated to him, then at best 40 percent of your portfolio is earning 3-4 percent per annum (pending interest rates).

When using the traditional model; it is *near impossible* to match markets for your overall portfolio, never mind beat them year in and year out.

It would be easy to play this down at this point and say that 'bonds aren't designed' to beat the performance of the FTSE 100 (as an example), but the reality is, as well as having a managed performance curve, you crave performance for your portfolio!!

Before fees, and due to the 'allocation model/diversification' referenced above, your 7 percent return might now have reduced to 4-5 percent. Let's call it 4.5 percent for this illustration.

Onto the fees (and this is where you might squirm a little): If you worked with one particular company who happen to be one of the UK's largest wealth managers (you might know who they are), you might have a fee structure that looks something like this:

1.5 percent yearly management fee.

1 percent fee per fund.

Let's offer them the benefit of the doubt and say their funds match market performance. However, due to the 60/40 allocation model, and now their fees, all of a sudden you might be looking at a return of around 3 percent (probably less) of the 7 percent market returns.

The difference over the years between a 3 percent annual return and a 7 percent compounded annual return is like night and day!

It may not seem like a lot but let me demonstrate why it most certainly is.

'Compounding' means getting a return on your investment to increase its total value, and then getting another return on that return. This 'compounding' effect increases the total value of your investment even more and the longer you are invested, the greater the impact.

The way compounding works on your investments is relatively simple. In the first year of investing, you may generate modest returns on the initial capital. Without withdrawing that money and leaving it invested, in the second year, you would have invested the original capital plus the returns you may have got from year one.

Imagine this being repeated over several years (though you are unlikely to get positive market returns every year) and so you unleash the potential to generate further returns on the total. And so, it goes on, helping you to build a bigger pot.

So, £100 invested receives 10 percent profit over one year, thereby growing to £110. The next year it's £110 generates 10 percent, thereby growing to £121.0. If the same thing kept happening over the next three years the investment would grow to £133.1, then £146.4, then £161.1. This happens because the returns remain invested, so they compound.

Compounding like this can be so powerful because this effect, in theory, is exponential. Even Albert Einstein is alleged to have noted that "compound interest is the most powerful force in the universe".

You may not achieve positive returns every year, although the probability of losing money has been historically proven to fall the longer you stay invested.

Patience is key to allowing compounding to work its magic over time, and if you stay invested over a longer term, you are giving your investments a better chance to make up for any short-term losses.

This is why compounding returns are so valuable to investors.

Let me show you what 15 percent per annum looks like over 15 years when your returns are compounded.

50K GBP portfolio starting point:

50K + 15% =57.5 K

57.5K + 15% =66.13 K

66.13K + 15% =76.04 K

76.04K + 15% =87.45 K

87.45K + 15% =100.57 K

100.57K + 15% =115.65 K

115.65K + 15% =132.998 K

133k + 15% =152.95 K

153k + 15% =175.95 K

176K + 15% =202.4 K

202.4K + 15% =232.76 K

232.76k + 15% =267.674 K

267.64K + 15% =307.786 K

307.78K + 15% =353.947 K

352.95K + 15% =405.893 K

After 15 years, a 50K GBP portfolio making a compounded 15% per annum would now be a 405,000 GBP portfolio.

250K GBP portfolio starting point:

250K + 15% =287.5 K

287.5K + 15% =330.625 K

330.63k + 15% =380.225 K

380.23K + 15% =437.265 K

437.27K + 15% =502.861 K

502.86K + 15% =578.289 K

578.29K + 15% =665.0335 K

665.03K + 15% =764.785 K

764.79K + 15% =879.509 K

879.51K + 15% =1,011.437 K

1011K + 15% =1,162.65 K

1163K + 15% =1,337.45 K

1337K + 15% =1,537.55 K

1538K + 15% =1,768.7 K

1769K + 15% =2,034.35 K

After 15 years, a 250K GBP portfolio making a compounded 15% per annum would now be a 2,034,035 GBP portfolio.

Although 15 percent per annum isn't a market return that is easy to achieve, by minimising the fees you pay, and making some subtle tweaks to your portfolio structure, it is possible. It's what most people reading this book should be working towards.

However, let's not get side tracked to where we might be in the future, and stay with our wealth management portfolio example. If you had a portfolio worth 250K GBP and over 15 years you made 3 percent per annum you would have 398K after the compounding impact.

Quite a difference to having a portfolio worth over 2m GBP.

If you had generated 7 percent per annum, your portfolio would now be worth 686,158 GBP.

If you could beat your market benchmark and generate just 10 percent per annum, you would now have 1,146,000 GBP in your portfolio…

Who says compounded growth doesn't work?

After a year or two of working with the traditional model, you might already see this lag in your investment curve, and you might want to leave your wealth manager. However, this is where you might receive a hefty shock.

Some wealth managers in the UK have fees of up to 5 percent to walk away!

Can you see why I am of the opinion that the traditional world of wealth management isn't designed to beat the markets for investors like you and me?

Now don't get me wrong, I'm not saying you can't make money with this model, you can. I'm not saying as a long-term growth model it can't work (to some extent), but I'm sure you can see the underlying problems here.

However, please also bear in mind, your typical wealth manager knows next to zero about 'market timing'.

They take your money, and they place it into the markets.

Again, it's ludicrous that very little thought goes into the timing of your entry point, but let's be candid, it's a reality.

Therefore, what happens when you follow the above approach (like most investors at the moment) and you hand over your hard-earned wealth to your IFA is that they place your investment straight into the markets at whatever price the market is offering on that day, and often near highs.

Even amateur investors are aware that markets don't increase in value in a straight line, and if your wealth manager with his one tactic (buy and hold) places your pool of money into the market before a 10 percent retracement, a 15 percent retracement, or God forbid a 20 percent retracement, can you imagine how long it might take just to get your portfolio back to break even?

Again, I will reiterate:

Even when using a wealth manager where the fees are substantially less (there are lots of them) I still believe it is almost impossible to consistently beat your market benchmark year in and year out.

The reality is, the model we're bred to believe is the only way to invest, is really built for the shareholders of the wealth managers. Not the clients and investors like you and me.

A scenario to ponder over:

A large fund might have 150 BILLION GBP under management. If they charged their customers 1.5 percent per year regardless of market climate, and regardless of their own performance and regardless of the returns for clients, where is the incentive for them to change the stale and outdated model that they've had in place for decades that has made many a shareholder and employee extremely wealthy?

It is possible you might encounter a friendly market climate. A stock market that might continue to increase in value, and despite entering around the highs your portfolio still might increase in value. However, don't worry, these greedy wealth managers will capture a large portion of that growth with their 'profit fees'.

Ultimately, however you slice and dice this model, it is not designed to help you nor me .

My partner and I met Paul Lindsay a number of years ago. Paul has been an IFA for over two decades. One of the nicest guys you'll ever meet but he'll be the first to tell you that the model he has been chained to for over 20 years is one that has afforded him little flexibility for his clients, and their allocations.

For his own investments, Paul wanted something different.

He considered investing on a DIY platform, even wondering whether there were IFAs out there who had more flexibility than him.

Despite working as an IFA for over two decades, he shared many of the same frustrations we all have.

Finally, he took the plunge and started to work with the strategies we'll be describing in this book. He's never looked back.

Here is what Paul had to say:

'Having access to these strategies is like having access to the best traders in the world. I am consistently beating my market benchmark'.

If these strategies can transform the investment portfolio of a career IFA, imagine what they can do for mere mortals.

WHY PASSIVE STRATEGIES DON'T WORK AS WELL AS THEY SHOULD, AND HOW YOU CAN MODIFY THIS APPROACH.

I mentioned earlier that as well as the extortionate fees and the 'diversification allocation' model that IFAs follow, that you might already be 3-4 percent behind global equity market performance every year.

Another thing I touched on that is worth elaborating further is 'the timing of building a portfolio' with a wealth manager.

It's slightly harsh of me to say this, but in my humble opinion most (not all) IFAs are salesmen, not market experts. It's only one man's viewpoint.

They follow an allocation model which often restricts what they can invest into. They take as much fees as they can, and once you're in the market, they're onto the next client.

Like I said, it's a harsh outlook, but one I feel quite strongly about when it comes to 'most' IFAs (I exclude some contacts I have made over the years who are excellent IFAs in a very restricted world).

The part of their approach where they 'place the money into the market and then move on' really needs to be looked at.

Why not stagger the entry over several months? Why not enter after every small pullback? Yes, it is a little bit more work, but if your client and their wealth growing is your number one priority, then it's certainly worth doing.

It's one of the main reasons why passive strategies don't work as well as they should. Changes need to be made to the model, and some of the frameworks within this book will teach you how to make the tweaks yourself.

After all, it doesn't have to be like this. You don't have to invest into a broken model.

Adam chose not to. I met Adam on the school playground at our children's school.

Adam is a super successful and intelligent individual (and all-round brilliant guy) but due to time constraints he was unable to manage his own portfolio. He had grown frustrated with the underperforming and over paid wealth managers. He felt trapped.

Whilst maintaining his current holdings, he wanted to know more about how we approached the markets. After a couple of conversations, Adam was convinced. He took the plunge. It's safe to say, he hasn't regretted his decision.

Here is what Adam had to say after working with these strategies:

'A refreshingly different approach to investing, and one that is outperforming my traditional investments.'.

The frameworks in this book will hopefully have the same results for you.

At this stage we've started to explore why the passive model doesn't work as well as it should. However, let's dig deeper. Over the next few pages, I'll explain some other reasons for the underperformance of the passive model, but much more importantly, we can start looking at the frameworks required to succeed.

LET ME START THIS WITH A STORY-

Over my career, I have spoken with tens of thousands of *passive* investors- and they all share the same frustrations you may feel.

They know that global stock markets increase in value every year, the statistics are there to verify this, but they also can't understand why they always lag the overall performance.

One person that really springs to mind here is a chap called Chris Pullen.

For decades the Pullen family had been building their family business. They're electricians and they serve their local area incredibly well. They're well respected, pillars of the community, and successful.

Chris (and his father before him) have been growing their business each and every year.

On the back of this, it has allowed them to invest a proportion of their earnings into the stock markets, to try and create a portfolio that builds their wealth for generations to come.

They hoped it would be a portfolio that would be passive, of a lower risk, and able to generate results comparable to markets.

About ten years ago, when Chris was comfortable with the mechanics of the business, and how it operated day to day, he wanted to look deeper into their family investment portfolio, and the performance of it. He wanted to find out where it could improve and what the weaknesses were.

At that stage they worked with a financial advisor the family had known for decades, but when he compared the performance of their portfolio v's the general market performance, he couldn't quite comprehend what his analysis was telling him.

The MSCI world index generated 12 percent in a thriving year. However, in those same years, the Pullen family were yielding on average about 8 percent. Does this tale sound familiar?

An average year for the global stock market index was about 6-7 percent over the time period he studied, but the Pullen family made closer to 3-4 percent. To Chris, it just didn't make sense.

At first, he thought that perhaps his calculations were wrong, but as he sifted through the numbers, the pattern repeated over and over.

10 percent for the MSCI, 6.4 percent for their portfolio, 8.4 percent for the MSCI, 5.1 percent for their portfolio.

It rumbled on and the theme was very consistent.

How could this be?

They had built a portfolio that didn't take on excessive risk, they had a portfolio structured to capture market movements, yet they seemed to always lag global stock market by a consistent 2-4 percent per annum. It wasn't just over a year or two; it was the same every year.

It was safe to say Chris found this frustrating, but it might also be a story that many reading this book today can relate too.

Now as an optimist myself, I don't like doom and gloom, so let me provide you with the good news. One day the penny dropped for Chris. He started to read around, he actively reached out to and conversed with investors who had experience of beating their market benchmark, and many familiar themes resurfaced.

In fact, he concluded that maybe it wasn't his advisor who was poor or made the wrong decisions, maybe it was the *wealth management model* that was letting him down.

He knew he had to make the changes, and he did. Traditions that had served the Pullen family relatively well had to be modified. False beliefs had to be broken down.

In a relatively short space of time, Chris went from lagging the market every year by 3-4 percent, to performing closely to his benchmark. It was quite the change.

He realised that this wealth management game wasn't as complicated as he had been informed, and that by taking more control, by taking the power back, and by making some subtle tweaks, that his performance and therefore the wealth of his family, could increase substantially. The roadblocks that had been getting in their way, were smashed out of the way. It was a great start to a portfolio transformation and evolution.

However, Chris wanted more (and why not), and by reaching out to us about four years ago, his portfolio not only matches the general stock market performance, but also beats his benchmark consistently, thanks to the exact tactics and strategies that I will teach you the frameworks for within this book.

However, where did it start going right for Chris and his investment portfolio, and what were the changes he made to execute the dramatic reversal?

Earlier in this book, I stated that there are mitigating factors caused by the 'wealth management model' that can reduce your investment portfolio's performance. Chris worked these out for himself after extensive analysis of his portfolio's performance over the years.

The mitigating factors discussed already are very big factors to why investors globally are constantly underperforming, but there are more we are yet to even discuss. Let's push on.

I'll start by looking at the **why**.

Why is a performance like this so very typical of a passive investor, and what can you do to change this status quo?

History informs us that global stock markets increase in value year on year. Yet often, you will invest at the wrong time. Therefore, this makes passive investment performance very hard to maximise.

Even if you are lucky enough to 'time it right' (potentially after a large market pullback), as I previously referenced, the wealth management model takes from your gains with fees, fees and more fees.

More importantly, although the concept of passive investing sounds great, the reality is that global stock markets are very volatile. Therefore, investors often have to deliberate as to when they should add capital into the markets.

How can they adopt an approach that makes passive investing work better?

How do they know that the market rally they're witnessing is a prudent time to move into cash?

How do they know when they should remove their chips off the table and take their profits?

Let's be fair; they probably don't, and as a reader of this book you probably don't either.

This is why passive investing is such a struggle. Indecision, uncertainty, and generally, a yearly return that underperforms simple market trackers.

Now the reality of the situation is that over the longer term, with the right tweaks, and the right guide, **a passive investing approach can and should form part of your overall portfolio structure.** However;-

You have to invest at the right time.

You have to invest by yourself (to ensure the fees remain low and your performance is as close to market performance as is possible).

If an investor ensures that these two variables are in place and working correctly, then passive investing can certainly form part of your portfolio. However, the positive news is, this book and the frameworks inside it can demonstrate the rest.

Even with the traditional passive investing model you will manage to accrue some growth (which for some is absolutely fine), but with a twist on how you utilise passive strategies, and by adopting a low-cost approach that is better timed, your passive approach could perform so much better.

I can't stress enough that even if you do 'time the entry' right with the traditional model, the fees on the fees will soon catch up with you and your portfolio performance!

Over the last few years, global stock markets have been very volatile. As much as an IFA might hide from this, volatility does create opportunity.

If you liked a stock or a particular stock market index one week ago, and due to no other reason other than excessive market volatility you're offered that same stock or market at a 5 percent lower valuation a week later, surely that's the time to enter for the long term?

Look, without beating 'passive investing' up too badly, let me end by suggesting that over the long term it can form a great *part* of your overall portfolio. However, you need to ensure you invest yourself and improve your market timing (e.g. after a market retracement).

If you read this book and put into action nothing else apart from the above, my job here is done. Mission accomplished. However, I am only scratching the surface of what you could potentially do.

Make no bones about it, the two tiny tweaks I have referenced here will save you a substantial amount of capital each and every year, and your portfolio will grow far more than previously.

The above modifications may well assist you in building a portfolio that is more aligned with general 'market performance'. However, if you are the type of individual who is prepared to dig deeper and are keen to enter the world of 'market beating performance' then fortunately for you, you're reading the right book.

Over the rest of this book, I will show you how to build a portfolio that aims to beat your market benchmark consistently.

In fact, let me tell you about Manu Sareen. Like many investors we have assisted, Manu has had a portfolio for a couple of decades. He's a business owner, he's successful, and from an investment point of view, he's always been a little frustrated. In fact, when I first met Manu at an investment show he informed me how little he rated the wealth management model, how he thought the wealth managers were substantially overpaid, and frankly, how he was disappointed in his lifetime ROI.

If you are beginning to understand how I think from reading this book, you would know the above was music to my ears and instantly, I was keen to assist him..

After working out what his objectives were, Manu went to work in the markets with the strategies we had designed.

The results were there for all to see, and bit by bit his frustrations left him.

In fact, Manu said the following recently:

'Knowledgeable and professional team and very happy to recommend their strategies.'

Like I said before and to reiterate, these strategies have worked for experienced investors, they've worked for inexperienced investors and most importantly of all- they could also work for you.

We hope you've enjoyed the insight provided so far, absorbed the expensive lessons we have already learned, built a better understanding of why the outdated wealth management model is failing all of us, and are already considering making some subtle tweaks and modifications to your portfolio approach referenced in this book. However, this book is about to move through the gears.

In these next three chapters, you'll learn the three insider tactics and techniques used by successful investors and traders (like the ones showcased on TPP) which minimises losses and helps investors to beat their market benchmark. We'll also help you understand why these techniques are not common knowledge.

If you were looking for some granular detail, then the following three chapters are exactly what you've been waiting for.

HOW TO BUILD A MARKET BENCHMARK BEATING PORTFOLIO: A TRACKER WITH A TWIST.

Remember earlier I told you about the framework we had developed that helped me to find a way to consistently beat my market benchmark without the need for my wealth manager? Let me explain this framework to you. I call it 'The three techniques to change how you invest forever' and I'll start with an adaptation on a simple index tracker.

Technique 1- A TRACKER WITH A TWIST (OR TWO).

I will state right now that there are very few people who are **bigger fans of buying and holding equities than I am.**

They are without doubt one of the most amazing wealth growing tools in the world

OVER THE YEARS WE HAVE WITNESSED THE FOLLOWING RETURNS:

THE FTSE 100 in the UK 5.2 percent per annum.

EUROPEAN INDICES 6.8 percent per annum.

US INDICES 7.2 percent per annum.

With compounded growth, and as a long-term growth tool they are very hard to beat.

However, you certainly don't need to pay your IFA or wealth manager 2-3 percent per annum to build this type of exposure for you.

Therefore, it's a very logical solution. Eliminate the wealth manager and their fees and very quickly, your performance increases, your portfolio growth changes, and most importantly of all, your wealth compounds far quicker than ever before.

If you follow these two simple tactics I'll outline, it will convert a tracker that tracks the market, into one that beats your benchmark consistently.

In simple terms it will make passive investing work far better than ever before.

First Tracker Twist Tactic:

Add 1.5 x leverage when linking with a market index.

Let me ask you a question:

Would you rather generate 7 percent per annum or 10.5 percent per annum by following the exact same stock market?

I assume you'll answer the latter, and this is exactly what you can do, by adding a sprinkling of leverage to your portfolio, and the market index that you're following as a long-term play.

Before implementing this modification on your portfolio, it is very important to know that leverage in the wrong hands is a wrong and dangerous investment tool.

There are many retail brokers that will offer investors just like you the ability to leverage your exposure by 100 or even 500 x. Please, never do this. There is a reason why most of these brokers in question have over 70 percent of investors who lose money that work with them, and that's because a retail investor tends to overexpose themselves with a level of leverage a professional would never consider.

However, leverage in the hands of a highly skilled investor, it is an absolutely invaluable investment tool.

By adding 1.5 x leverage (no more is required) into your long-term growth plays like the FTSE 100, SP500, Dow Jones etc, it can improve their per annum performance considerably.

Pre Trump Tariffs, US markets were thriving. Can you imagine as well as catching every movement whilst they thrive, but also compounding that gain by 1.5 x every year?

That is the power of leverage.

As well as this, by not overextending your exposure and by retaining leverage at 1.5 x or lower, it should ensure that your volatility is also well within your comfort levels. As an example, in a Covid/credit crunch type situation you could witness stocks decrease in value by as much as 20 percent. You need to be aware that by leveraging yourself by 1.5 x, that your volatility will also be increased by 1.5 x. Therefore, on these rare occasions where in the short-term markets drop and depreciate by 20 percent, could you handle that short term retracement being 1.5 x higher at 30 percent?

If the answer to that is YES, then a sprinkling of leverage is a must for your portfolio.

The key words here are 'a sprinkling'. This is where some investors go wrong.

Leverage of 3-4 x may not seem massively out of sync with your risk appetite when markets are tracking in the right direction (like they often do), but it will feel very different in those rare occasions when the markets drop like a stone.

Don't put this level of stress on yourself. It isn't required.

Sprinkle your portfolio with a touch of leverage, accept there will be a little more volatility, and yield 1.5 x market performance each and every year.

Unless you have zero appetite for any risk, a small amount of leverage will completely change your investment performance.

Your IFA probably wouldn't even know how to employ leverage on your portfolio, most have never placed a trade in their careers. They allocate their money to wealth managers and leave the trading decisions to the traders of the funds.

I'm telling you today that *any* investor with a little experience can add a touch of leverage to their portfolio, and providing it's used correctly and in small doses, it will change your portfolio performance completely. With this technique we're only just getting started.

Are you ready for further portfolio structure improvements? In that case, let's explore the second tactic to this tracker approach.

Second Tracker Twist Tactic:

I hope you can already ascertain that by supplementing your long-term equity index trackers with a touch of leverage, it should be enough to turbo charge your trading performance. I regularly inform my friends and family that although the world of investing is made to sound complicated, if you understand it, and the instruments available to investors like you and I, its actually far less complex than many believe.

If markets yield 6-7 percent per annum, with 1.5 x leverage you'll be generating 9-10.5 percent in that very same year. What about those over performing years where global stocks generate 12-15 percent? Imagine how different your portfolio performance will look in those years?

Again, the power of a small amount of leverage is hard to understand if you've never been exposed to it; It's very real and it's available to *all* investors.

However, like I touched on earlier it also adds an extra layer of volatility.

This next tactic in my opinion helps to mitigate that volatility and downside risk, and in my experience, it tends to compound the growth potentially even quicker. Excited?

Let me explain the details behind this approach, but beforehand the tactic headline:

Always add a small position when markets pull back 5 percent from highs.

This might sound simple, but you wouldn't believe how much this improves your portfolio performance. This might even compound your gains quicker than the 1.5 x leverage.

Together, these two easy to understand tactics will help a basic tracker strategy (which is also now minus the fees) consistently beat their market benchmarks year after year, and I would expect based on the structure of these approaches, that they'll beat the benchmarks by at least 1.5 x and provide a great long-term growth structure for your portfolio.

With these basic frameworks and the modifications you can implement with your portfolio, you will completely change your overall portfolio performance, and your wealth growth could become dramatic.

I hope you can visualise how different your portfolio structure could become, and how you will have limited reliance on your wealth manager or IFA moving forward.

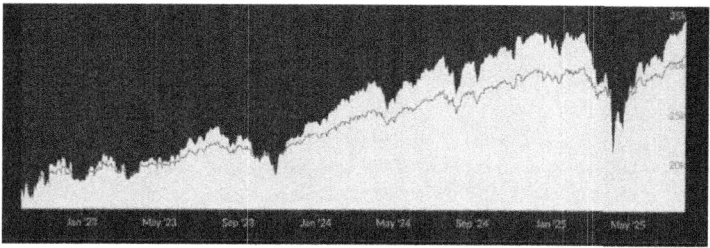

OUTPERFORMING MARKETS EVERY YEAR:

Browse the above to see the performance of this strategy. It is based on our TPP platform, and you can clearly see its outperformance vs general market performance. The line within the bolded performance chart (this strategy performance) is the performance of the S&P. This is the type of performance you will have the ability to aspire towards by utilising the frameworks described.

HOW TO BUILD A MARKET BENCHMARK BEATING PORTFOLIO: THE LONG OR FLAT APPROACH.

Technique 2: Even if you ceased reading this book right now, even with the limited teachings offered, and the frameworks shared, I would expect that you would be able to build a portfolio that more than likely would consistently beat your market benchmark.

I really hope you can visualise this. If so, then my explanations are of the required standard. If this is the case, then you're possibly also thinking that it is a tad crazy that you now have this knowledge and ability at your fingertips, whilst many investors (and wealth managers) struggle to beat their benchmark over a 30-year investing career.

Like I said earlier, the world of investing can become very complex if you let it. However, if you understand how to approach the markets, how to keep it simple, and how to utilise the investment instruments available to us, then it really isn't rocket science. You just need to understand simple market dynamics. Don't let your wealth manager tell you otherwise or let them inform you how much you need them. Didn't Blockbusters used to say the same about requiring them to watch movies? We know how that one ended.

However, as impressive as the 'tracker with the twist (or two)' is, this next technique–**The Long or Flat– is what** I would describe this approach as the next level for your portfolio.

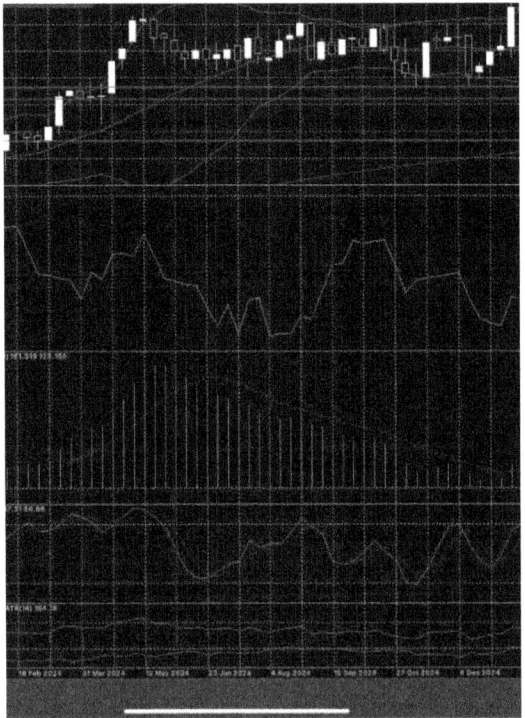

To describe how we would employ this approach, I've included a chart of our stock market in the UK; The FTSE 100. This illustration is over roughly a 12-month time period.

126

We referenced earlier that over its history, it averages around 5.2 percent per annum. A steady and solid return, without being one of the higher performers.

However, it is very clear that it certainly doesn't increase in value in a straight line. Far from it. Over time it tends to deliver.

Just before moving into the minutiae of this technique, let's recall where the land lies at this stage with our new level of knowledge. As of right now, we have the knowledge and understanding to build a portfolio with our slightly leveraged trackers. With these in place **to capture every movement, and every profitable year, and by also adding small increments to our exposure after market retracements**, we are already in a very sound place. We could leave it at that. However, the fact that you're reading on suggests to me that you're thirsty for more, so let me deliver that for you. In fact, if you're not overwhelmed yet then it's time for us to gain an understanding of the second technique to assist you to build your very own market beating portfolio.

THE LONG OR FLAT: Markets often trade in ranges. Although they typically move up over the longer term, they don't increase in value in straight lines. This is obvious to anyone with a passing interest in the investment world. However, did you know that with subtle tweaks to our portfolio structure and approach we can take advantage of these ranges?

Let me explain how.

In very simple terms, when a stock market looks like it might reside in over bought territory, we can move into a FLAT/ MARKET NEUTRAL POSITION and wait for a market retracement in order to move back into the market on the BUY side.

The reason why we do this is to capture the bulk of the movement when markets move in an upward trajectory, but more importantly, to avoid portions of small market retracements which happen on a regular basis.

Think about this logically. Even if we miss 0.5 percent of a market retracement, that's a further gain come year end with our portfolio.

Miss it on 10-12 occasions over a period of a year, and that's an extra 5-6 percent in our pockets…

Of course, there will be occasions when we move flat, and markets push forward and higher than our exit point, but by following these tactics consistently, you'll miss far more retracements than you will miss highs that become higher highs. Also, with the entry points outlined below even if markets do move a touch higher at first, it won't be long until we're back in the markets and riding that trend.

Once we've decided to move our investment in a particular market into a market neutral/flat position, the conditions to buy back into the same market are simple. Etch this one into your trading mindset: When markets pull back a minimum of 1 percent from when we moved into a flat position/previous highs- WE BUY BACK IN.

Sounds simple, but it works!

You might be thinking about how this seems like it could work, but wondering when you should move into a market neutral position, and how you should determine over bought territory? If you are, then you're on the right track. That is what you should be asking yourself right now.

That's what I'm here for. To provide you with the solutions. To offer working examples to the theory and to assist you to implement these approaches. The answer to your question is this: There are a few key conditions we follow for the 'set up' of this type of trade.

The Long or Flat conditions are the following:

CONDITIONS TO GO FLAT ARE EITHER:

A) The RSI indicator is over 70, and the momentum indicators are turning down. Or;

B) The price action is touching the top level of our bollinger band. Or:

C) The ATR has moved 1.5X its daily range in 1 day, and the price action is above the 50-day moving average. Or:

D) The price action is within 1 percent of the top level of the bollinger band, and the momentum indicators have turned down.

At this stage, we would move into a flat/market neutral position.

Following the above guide, we've now managed to exit the market, and hopefully at a solid exit point. However, we're probably also sitting there wondering when we should move back into the market, and you should be, so let me explain and assist:

Buy back in after any retracement as much as 1 percent (ideally more) in the index you have exited.

Once your position is back in the market, never go flat/market neutral again for at least 7 days to allow the conditions to adjust.

When looking for an exit or entry point, check the market conditions/prices once or twice a day at the same time. Be consistent with this!.

That is the set-up, the entry and the exit points for our long or flat strategies.

As you can see for yourself, it's slightly more complex than our first technique, but an excellent strategy to deploy if you have the time to monitor the markets a couple of times on a daily basis. When I say a couple of times, I mean no more than checking the price action for five minutes twice per day.

My expectations for this framework are relatively high.

In fact, I would expect this to achieve slightly more than your leveraged tracker (pending market conditions) as you will hopefully miss many of the sharp market retracements.

However, together they are quite the powerhouse of approaches.

At this stage of the book, do you still think you need your IFA to manage all of your investments? (You don't need to answer that one).

I am passionate about letting investors know that there are better ways to invest, that they can build approaches that will consistently beat their market benchmarks but at the same time, without the reliance on their wealth managers and IFAs. However, it is one thing saying it and quite another demonstrating it. Some people *talk* about beating market benchmarks, while some actually *do* beat market benchmarks. Have a look at the chart below. This is a 'long or flat' strategy over the last five years. Yet again, you can also see the performance of a strong S&P 500 over the same period.

Can Long or Flat strategies assist you to beat your market benchmark?

I'll let you be the judge of that.

OUTPERFORMING MARKETS EVERY YEAR

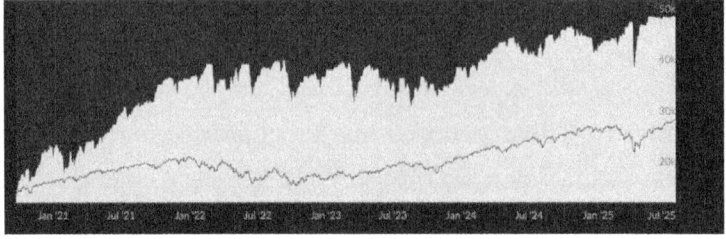

The information you have been reading and digesting over these chapters might be a lot to take in and absorb. However, use this book as your 'investing toolbox' that you can revert to at any time. Once you've utilised these techniques on a few occasions, they'll become as easy as riding a bicycle.

You now have the knowledge, guidelines and frameworks to build a portfolio exactly like the one in the illustration. How does your portfolio performance compare in the same time period? Again, you don't need to answer that.

Change is necessary, and this book will help you to make the modifications required.

By following these two tried and tested techniques, you can build the portfolio that you've always craved. The one that doesn't lag, the one that doesn't underperform year in and year out, and the one that doesn't come with never ending excuses from your IFA. Now is your time.

The two techniques described are 'your portfolio foundations', and again, if you stopped reading right here you would have enough knowledge to go and improve

your performance dramatically. However, if you want even more let's dive even deeper again!

Beforehand, I just want to reiterate that these two techniques are all that is needed, and for many investors reading this book they will be more than enough, but this third technique for those that want to take their investing even further, might even be the icing on your investing cake.

HOW TO BUILD A MARKET BENCHMARK BEATING PORTFOLIO: THE ACTIVE EQUITY LONG OR SHORT STRATEGY.

Technique 3: This is the active equity long/short technique investment approach and for those who can stomach a little more risk and volatility, it's the speculative edge to your portfolio.

The coup de grace. Or some might even call it: The game changer for your portfolio. Let me explain:

Before we investigate this approach in forensic detail, there needs to be one large caveat stated. This is a more aggressive approach. This is a more volatile approach. This framework isn't for every investor.

However, executed well; it provides you with the edge that most investors won't have with their portfolio.

This strategy builds positions using the previous two techniques, but also looks to gain as the markets retrace. Yes, it looks to make money as markets fall.

Like I said, it's not for everyone.

Combine this approach and framework with the other two techniques, and although it is only one man's opinion, I believe that you will be able to build a world class benchmark beating portfolio structure. An investment approach that would be the envy of many a hedge fund.

However, let's drop the hyperbole and focus on the actual framework as you're probably wondering what the conditions are to implement this technique?

Yet again, I'm here to assist.

When utilizing this approach, you will be *buying the market* using the same techniques described for the other predominantly *long/buy* strategies previously detailed. Please don't forget to add to your *long* exposure with this strategy. However, as well as combining opportunities on the *buy* side, where this really separates itself from the other approaches is its ability to *short/sell the market*.

Therefore, as we already know the different situations where we would *buy* with this framework, let's focus on how we may be able to profit on a market retracement.

These are the conditions required to implement a short sell position:

(EITHER):

A) The RSI indicator is above 80 (eighty), which suggests that the market you are analysing is very overbought.

However, we also need a second guide using the entry point. We also need the momentum indicators to be turning down. There is no point selling a market just because it's high. We need the confirmation that the momentum is reversing.

B) The price action is 1 percent above the top level of our bollinger band. This suggests extreme overbought conditions, and we can take a calculated risk that momentum is about to reverse, and enter before the confirmation. :

C) The ATR indicator has moved up 1.5X its daily range in 1 day, and the price action is below the 200 day moving average. This suggests we're selling at a recent high and close to the high of the day, and that the overall trend is still down (200DMA). It is an excellent set up for a short/sell entry point. .

With any of these set ups, you could enter a short/sell position.

With a framework and approach like this, you should aim to have a risk to reward ratio of 2.5:1. Set stops 1 ATR away, with a profit stop 2.5 ATR away. .

To provide a further depth on this, if the ATR (average daily movement range) is 100, then the stop should be 100 pips away, and the profit stop 250 pips away. You could also use this approach with a 1.2 ATR stop (120 pips away) and a profit stop 2.5 X 120.

Often when detailing these frameworks, I preach consistency, and it really is key.

You could have a successful methodology to build a benchmark beating portfolio, but if you aren't consistent with your implementation of it, your results will mimic your inconsistency. It doesn't really matter if you have your stop 1 ATR away or 1.2 ATR away, what does matter is that you're consistent with your choice.

Another key activity: Check the conditions once or twice a day at the same time of day/night. Again, to reiterate, you're not a day trader. You shouldn't want to be, and you don't need to be.

When you check the conditions, if you haven't hit either stop after five days, close the trade. We don't want to hold a short sell trade over the mid term when history informs us that equity markets typically increase in value.

Yes, money can be made within the market gyrations and retracements, but don't sit on a short sell waiting for a market crash. Even for experienced traders this is a hard approach to adopt as you need to constantly tweak your short sell position to stay in the game.

THE AIM WITH THIS APPROACH IS TO YIELD A RETURN AND MAKE MONEY ON SMALL RETRACEMENTS IN THE MARKET YOU ARE ANALYSING IN VERY OVER BOUGHT CONDITIONS, AND WHEN OTHER FACTORS ARE IN YOUR FAVOUR (EG MOMENTUM, TREND ETC).

As a successful trader or investor, we should aim to play a high probability game. We don't like guesses; we don't like 50/50's. Like a skilled poker player, we make our move when the probabilities are in our favour. This doesn't mean we win every trade. That's impossible. However, we have a methodology that is set up to succeed, we take our losses, but we win far more often than not. Overall, we build a benchmark beating portfolio.

Combined with the first two techniques outlined already, this third technique whilst more sophisticated, can add gains to your portfolio that you wouldn't be able to achieve otherwise. However, like everything when it comes to investing, it's worth laying out a few simple caveats to apply at all times...

Do not use this technique *alone*.

Only use a little portion of your portfolio when on the short side.

Every little gain is a bonus on the short side.

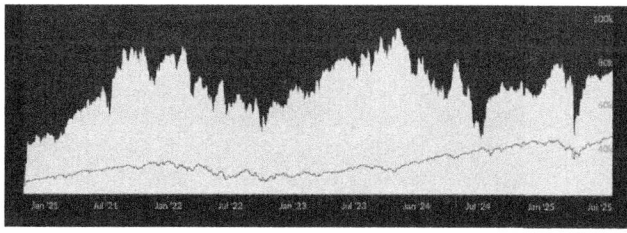

This above illustration shows an active equity long/short strategy. As I suggested earlier, these are more aggressive, they are more volatile, and they're also not for every investor.

However, if you think your risk appetite is compatible with this approach, then you have the keys to a portfolio structure that should purr like a finely tuned sports car engine.

I've included the performance of the S&P500 against this type of strategy to illustrate the power of an active equity long/short strategy.

What are your thoughts? Is this the type of approach you could adopt?

It isn't for everyone, but if you think it is for you, I expect it won't be a decision you regret in the future.

SUMMARISING THESE THREE INVESTMENT FRAMEWORKS.

The approach I have provided you with the frameworks for today is your key to beating your market benchmark. It's your way to either dispense with your underperforming IFA or wealth manager for good, or perhaps ensure you rely on them far less.

Far too many investors underperform their market benchmark. This book and the approach detailed is your key to beating yours.

In my opinion, once you read these chapters two or three times, you'll develop the understanding to build three benchmark beating techniques that stand a strong probability of delivering for you each year.

To summarise, technique one follows global stock markets closely. As a long-term growth tool, it is very hard to rival. The approach focuses on building portfolios that follow markets as they increase in value most years, therefore increasing the yearly return for your investment portfolio. It will have a touch more volatility than markets, but will consistently outperform them by close to (or more than) 1.5 x. This approach on its own would be enough to completely change your portfolio performance. This framework would allow you to build a portfolio your IFA or wealth manager would look at with envy. They probably wouldn't even be able to work out the subtle tweaks and modifications you were implementing for such dramatic impact.

Technique two is a little more advanced, but the trade-off for the slightly more monitoring that is required is worth it. This framework is designed to smooth out some of the volatility of the leveraged trackers by missing the occasional retracement (or part of them), and I would hope and expect it will also out deliver the performance of the leveraged tracker approach.

Remember, the leveraged tracker approach is built to outperform markets by 1.5 x. No if's, no buts. It will do exactly what it says on the tin, and that's before even adding a further increment/touch of leverage after a retracement.

Can you imagine how delighted/ecstatic you would be if those were the level of returns that your wealth manager delivered every year?

So even if the second framework 'only' delivers a similar return it will also be providing you with a touch of diversification in your approach.

Some investors might read this book, and just work with framework one. That is enough. Others might want to build the diversified profile of approach 1 and 2.

If that is the direction you take with your portfolio from this day on, the foundations you are building will be incredibly strong.

In fact, it might even be time to wave goodbye to your wealth manager.

As for technique three, it's a potential game changer, but if anything within its structure makes you slightly uncomfortable, then step aside. You need to know who you are as a person and an investor, and if the occasional short sell doesn't suit your investing psychology, then this tactic isn't for you. Do what makes you feel comfortable.

However, whether you use just one of the frameworks, the first two, or all three, I would expect you'll build a portfolio that performs like never before.

I'll be on the sidelines cheering you on. You've got this.

You now have the ammunition and the knowledge to build a portfolio that aims to yield 1.5 x your market benchmark consistently.

You now have the keys to unlock the chains that have been tied around your investment portfolio, and I for one look forward to following your journey.

I hope you can see that with subtle tweaks and modifications we have taken a portfolio that tracks the markets, into one that beats it consistently.

However, before you rush off and start tweaking your portfolio, let me tell you about SIMON:

In fact, Simon's results could probably articulate this far better than I ever could.

Simon was exposed to active equity long/short strategies a few years back when the markets tumbled. It was a scary period of time for investors globally. Do you remember it?

Simon certainly does. 'He made 25 percent in a year when the MSCI world index fell 18.9 percent in the same year'.

I hope as we conclude this book, that these strategies can do something similar for you and your underperforming portfolio.

WHAT WE HAVE COVERED AND THE MISCONCEPTIONS WE HAVE ELIMINATED.

Before moving forward, let's recap what we have learnt so far in this book– your very own trading toolbox.

We have addressed the big lie that your wealth manager has been selling you and how lining his or her pockets is crippling your performance. Can you see why we're bred to believe their model is the only one?

I have shown you today that it certainly isn't. I hope you can see that and understand the changes and modifications that need to be made.

We have also explored why passive strategies don't work as well as they should, and what you need to know to build a market benchmark beating portfolio each and every year. I'll be the first to confirm the relative merits of a passive approach. However, only with big caveats attached. We discussed these variables, and I hope you can understand why you need to 'time the market' better, and why you need to reduce your costs. Simple tweaks can have a dramatic impact. I hope you can see that with these simple modifications, you can start working towards market benchmark beating performance.

Finally, and probably most importantly of all, we have broken down the three insider tactics successful traders and investors use, and why they aren't common knowledge. This was the big one and was a lot of information to digest if you are looking to build a portfolio by using all three tactics. However, even just using just 1 of these techniques could help you to outperform your market benchmark. If you decided to utilise two of these approaches, then potentially you could build a structure that might result in substantial outperformance.

However, with all three techniques and frameworks, I hope you can see how you could potentially build a world class market benchmark beating portfolio which would be the envy of many.

I hope it's opened your eyes regarding how to implement the right changes, and how if you do, that they will change how you invest forever

If it has opened your eyes and mind, then suddenly beating your market benchmark consistently probably seems possible now. Perhaps even beating it by 1.5 X might seem within the realms of possibilities at this point? Remember, as ambitious as that statement sounds, the leveraged trackers we referenced are built to do exactly this. No if's, no but's.

What are you thinking right now?

Can you see the possibilities that are opening right in front of your eyes?

Here's the bottom line, and I think you probably already know this.

You can't afford to keep on investing like you do. Change is required. If you haven't beat your benchmark most years in your investing lifetime, then this toolbox is here to assist.

So let me ask you a question:

If you followed what I showed you in the first framework (leveraged tracker and buy the dip) and started to improve your portfolio performance almost instantly, then you used what I showed you in the second framework and used the long or flat strategy to really compound your gains, and then you utilised the third framework (active long/short) to add a more aggressive edge that aims to perform regardless of market climate, do you think you could be successful?

I certainly hope so.

I will follow that with another question:

Are you excited about my teachings in this book? Can you visualise the 'easy wins' already?

However, I do appreciate that for some it may have been a lot of information to digest. Perhaps you can understand how this could work for you, but as of right now you might be feeling a little overwhelmed? To be forthright, I could see why that might be the case for some, as we have covered a lot of information and approaches to the market.

Does the latter resonate with anyone reading this book today?

If you are feeling like that right now, 'don't worry'. Yet again, I have you covered.

In fact, from here I would say depending on your thoughts regarding implementing the required changes, you probably have two options ahead of you, and the positive news is, I think both of them will result in a better performing portfolio for you.

YOUR TWO OPTIONS.

In life, many options present themselves to you. Some people take decisive action, whilst others procrastinate. Some make instant decisions whilst others pontificate. Right now, in my humble opinion, you have two options available to you in your investment journey.

Option One: This book provides some easy-to-understand frameworks to assist you to improve your portfolio performance. This option involves you taking these frameworks, implementing them yourself, and improving your portfolio performance very quickly. In other words, you take today's findings and attempt to make these work for yourself. For many this will be the right option.

Read the techniques, read them again, absorb and digest them, and start to make the tweaks one by one.

Start with how you can save on fees, think about your diversification and whether you need as much cash/bonds allocation as you have, and then look to add our three techniques and frameworks one by one.

You won't change things overnight, but by taking your time, and making small tweaks I would expect you to notice material changes to your portfolio, what you're paying for it, and how it's over performing (vs markets) within 60-90 days.

You will face some challenges, a dab of adversity, a touch of pressure, and sometimes you may even doubt what you're doing.

However, stick with the course. Trust the process.

You'll make far less mistakes than I ever have (hopefully none) and please analyse your approach to the markets regularly.

No one is asking you to watch your portfolio constantly. In fact, you want to set the structures up and almost leave it.

However, time and patience will be required at first when making the changes you know you require.

Some things in life are easy but changing how you've always invested will take time.

In that time, the results will speak for themselves.

Good luck. I have every faith.

Option Two: You can visualise the changes needed, you are prepared to make them to your portfolio structure, however you feel a little overwhelmed. You're wondering if you could implement them as required, or whether it would be more advantageous to find yourself a guide who can assist you to implement these findings and condense your learning curve. For some, this would be the better approach, and a very fast and easy methodology to end your years of investing frustrations and underperformance.

Regarding the second option; What would it do for you if you gained a more thorough understanding than you have right now?

You know the basics; you can visualise that beating your market benchmark is possible. However, it may seem a little like 'information overload'.

If you now know that there are people (lots of them) who are consistently beating their market benchmark, or perhaps even yielding 1.5 x market returns, then every month you delay, you're losing. You're being left behind.

It is a harsh statement for me to make, but it is true. I hope you can see that.

YOUR GUIDE. A BONUS FOR MY BOOK READERS.

I hope this book becomes an Amazon best seller. It will provide me with great satisfaction if this book falls into the hands of as many frustrated investors around the globe as possible. I believe that the frameworks I've outlined in this book can be implemented by many investors themselves.

However, if you're a little unsure about how to implement the findings, rest assured that I can guide you.

As you've come this far in the book, you're already showing me that you're interested in finding ways to beat your market benchmark consistently. That in itself is massive. You're showing me that you understand that there are alternative, better and cheaper ways to the traditional model of wealth management.

As a thank you, I'm going to go over a FREE (YES FREE) offer I have created for my book readers that will help you implement what we've covered today.

I'll be candid. If the information you have read so far is enough, then feel free to skip forward to the free bonuses and resources I'm also providing you with (a must-read chapter) in this book.

If anyone doesn't want to learn this next part or find out more, that's totally fine. Skip forward now.

However, if you are keen to find out more, if you believe you'll need a guide to assist you to make these portfolio modifications (perhaps only initially), then here is something you may well be interested in.

For the right profile of investor; I want to offer you an opportunity.

I'm going to offer some of you a FREE session with either myself (time permitting) or my team.

On this call, I hope that you will leave with THE EXACT BLUEPRINT REQUIRED to beat your market benchmark consistently, and maybe even by 1.5 x per annum.

We will discuss your portfolio frustrations, we'll find out why it has been underperforming for so many years, we'll look at ways to fix it, and we will provide you with a plan and a guide to assist you to FINALLY end years of underperformance.

Sound like a prudent plan?

In fact, we did exactly the same for James Hicks.

James met us when he had lost faith with the traditional wealth management model and the 4-5 percent per annum he had been receiving over an extensive period of time. Like many of you, he was wondering if there was no other option. In his mind, he began to think that this stale model was destined to be for him forever.

He was wrong, and if you were thinking that before reading this book, so were you.

After working with our strategies and frameworks over the last few years, James had the following to say:

'Working with Lane and TPP is the best investment decision I have ever made'.

James has waved goodbye to 4-5 percent per annum, and now has a portfolio that consistently beats his benchmark.

Another quick story: This is a quick tale I like, and it's about Adam.

I was on holiday having a well-earned break in the sunshine when Adam scheduled a call via my electronic diary.

I thought I had booked the day off to spend time with the family, but I noticed there was a slot available, and Adam had taken it.

Once I apologized for the holiday attire (shorts and t-shirts), we chatted about the strategies we had built that we were now offering via our investment platform.

On the back of one call, Adam committed a touch under 1m GBP into these strategies.

It was safe to say: He was a believer.

Adam was from the wealth management industry. He had worked for hedge funds for his whole life, but he could see that what we had built was different, that these three tactics and frameworks really could help him to beat his market benchmark.

Thankfully, Adam's initial thoughts were right..

In fact, he stated that 'the world of wealth management is changing, and the strategies that TPP have built are at the forefront of this change.'

Adam, who are we to argue? We hope these three techniques continue to help you beat your benchmark for many decades to come.

Moving forward, I hope our market benchmark beating frameworks can do exactly the same for you.

As well as the other examples in this book, Gary is another great case study.

A property investor and entrepreneur, Gary had been struggling to find the best way to gain exposure to the financial markets for a number of years.

Just when he had lost nearly all hope, Gary was introduced to us by another one of our clients. Since he started working with us, Gary has changed how he approaches the markets and improved his performance dramatically.

In Gary's words:

'TPP and their strategies they have designed are far superior to other funds which charge high fees for nowhere near the return'.

We couldn't concur more.

Although it's great to hear about all of these success stories, the bottom line is this:

I want *you* to be next. I want you to build a market benchmark beating portfolio.

If you are the right profile of investor, and you're willing to make the required changes, I am confident that we could expedite your improvement curve for you.

However, before we get carried away, it would be prudent to ascertain whether you're the right fit for us, and perhaps more importantly, whether we're the right fit for you….

The only way we can understand that is by arranging a strategy session.

On the 'book purchaser bonus call', depending on how the conversation evolves, as well as having access to our frameworks and teachings from this book, you may also be offered a chance to work with us further.

I hope what we've taught you today is enough to improve your portfolio performance, but if you're ready to take that next step, and you're ready to make your portfolio modifications right now, then the bonus strategy session might open further doors for you and your investment portfolio performance.

However, working directly with us isn't for everyone, but we could certainly find out if it could be for you.

In fact, to potentially save both of our times, let me lay out exactly who these types of calls are for in case this is piquing your interest:

You are a frustrated investor who is ACTIVELY LOOKING to modify your approach and FINALLY beat your market benchmark.

You currently overpay for under performance.

You are DISILLUSIONED with the stale and outdated wealth management model. You know you need to make a change.

If this resonates with you, then there is a strong probability that you need our FREE strategy sessions!

So book your call now. Scan the QR code directly below and find out the exact blueprint required to build a portfolio that aims to consistently beat your market benchmark.

TPP: Schedule a call

VERY IMPORTANT:

If you decide to schedule a call, please **ensure** you complete the short form when booking your call. We tend to only have a few slots available most weeks, so the form will allow us to ensure you're the right type of investor that we believe we can assist, and we can help you to improve your portfolio performance.

On the call, as well as dissecting how you're investing right now, we may also offer you the opportunity to subscribe and link to some of our market benchmark beating strategies.

I would be incredibly confident in saying that I would expect that this will condense years of hard work and trial and error, into an **instant portfolio performance boost**.

However, to reiterate; These strategy calls are not for everyone.

If you're still reading this chapter, and haven't skipped forward to the FREE BONUS section, then there's a solid chance this type of call could be for you.

Now might be the time to end years of underperformance. It may indeed be the moment to build you a portfolio structure that aims to beat your benchmark and even yield 1.5 x market performance per annum.

If all of this is resonating, I can't stress enough:

APPLY FOR YOUR CALL RIGHT NOW…

TPP: Schedule a call

The world of wealth management is evolving. Find out if you could become part of our journey to change how the world invests.

We look forward to talking to you if you believe you're the right fit.

Your solution to your investment woes is far closer than you realise. When you learn the blueprint required to beat your market benchmark and the vehicles that can do it for you, you'll be able to change how you invest forever, and have far less reliance on your wealth manager or IFA.

When I was first figuring this out, I ran into many roadblocks. I didn't know how to beat my benchmark so I had to create the solution for myself.

For years, I had to go through a trading learning curve that cost me millions of GBP's and a lot of heartache to figure out an efficient way to handle this problem. I don't want you to have to recreate the wheel. I've already got this proven formula for you. All you need to do today is schedule a call.

When you use these three techniques and frameworks, you will save what could be months or years of wasted time and money because you'll be doing it right the first time. You'll have no trial-and-error period.

To conclude: If nothing else, I hope that after reading and digesting this book, that you'll take a serious look at your portfolio, the fees you pay and the changes you can make.

If you believe that you're the right fit for a free strategy call, what are you waiting for?

Schedule your call today!

Chapter 17

WRAPPING IT ALL UP (BEFORE THE FREE BONUSES).

I expect you might be thinking along the lines of this right now: 'Wow, that was a lot to take in. How am I going to implement all of that? However, the reality is, you don't need to implement everything, and definitely not all at once. Take a deep breath, relax, and read on.

What you read next might even assist you more than the 3 different approaches and frameworks. I also have a bundle of free gifts and resources to provide you with to assist you on your investment journey in the next chapter.

Ultimately if nothing else, this book was designed to open your eyes to how the wealth management model isn't designed to assist investors like you and me.

You may even agree that it's stale, it's outdated, and it's an industry that is ripe for disruption.

I hope so.

The more believers/advocates there are, the quicker this industry will change for the better.

You have now learned the key elements and strategies you need to create a market benchmark beating portfolio, and you've seen how making these tweaks and modifications could change your portfolio performance within the matter of 90 days.

Ensuring you make the modifications required to provide you with a solid portfolio structure, is the best investment you'll ever make in yourself.

It can be your secret to becoming the pride of your peers.

As a reminder- here is what we have covered:

Part #1 – The big lie that your wealth manager has been selling you and why lining his or her pockets is crippling your investments.

Part #2 - Why passive strategies don't work as well as they should, and how we can modify the approach to maximise our returns.

Part #3 – The 3 insider tactics most successful investors use to rarely lose and why it isn't common knowledge.

In my humble opinion you now have a number of tools/tweaks/ approaches that will assist you to improve your portfolio performance.

You may even decide to stick with what you've always done but work hard to drive your fees down. Any improvement from here is a good improvement.

However, I hope you take far more from this book.

I hope you consider implementing a couple of the tactics as a minimum that will help your underperforming portfolio evolve into one that beats its market benchmark consistently from here.

The industry is evolving, and by making the required changes you can be ahead of the curve of change.

So, let me ask you a few questions before heading to the free bonus section:

Was taking the time out to read this book worth it?

Can you now visualise that with a few simple tweaks to your portfolio structure that you *can* start to beat the general market performance?

Do you now understand why you don't need to rely on your wealth manager and/or IFA as much as you did, and you certainly don't need to pay their excessive fees?

Can you envisage making the changes required to build a better portfolio?

I hope you believe that beating the markets consistently or perhaps even by 1.5 x per annum is possible.

Change is required. You can't afford not to do so and fall further behind in your life goals.

Make the required modifications yourself or look for a market guide. If that guide happens to become TPP then know this:

Unlike wealth managers, we won't charge any management or performance fees.

Yes, you're right. We are different. We want to help investors just like you.

FINDING YOUR APPROACH, AND PORTFOLIO ALLOCATION.

The world of wealth management and yielding a better return for your portfolio on a per annum basis isn't rocket science. We are just led to believe it is.

The bottom line is that taking our portfolios away from our wealth managers or our financial advisors would in all likelihood boost all of our returns.

If you work with some of the more expensive wealth managers out there, then taking control of your portfolio will change the results so much you would barely believe it.

In this day and age when some of the largest wealth managers in the UK charge extortionate management fees, yearly fees on their *own* funds, performance fees, and exit and redemption fees, just putting your 'big boy investor' pants on and taking ownership would change the financial game for you.

This one change alone would save you thousands.

Then you're left with the dilemma of what to do with your portfolio next.

If you're looking at the financial markets, following the allocation models that most IFAs follow (60/40 stocks/bonds and cash) isn't the worst idea.

Yes, before anyone calls me out on this, I did say earlier in the book that blindly giving your capital to an expensive wealth manager and following their 60/40 allocation model doesn't make sense, and I will reiterate that, it doesn't. I'm not suggesting that. However, it is important to have some diversification, but if we can do that in a more effective manner, do it whilst paying less, and implement it alongside our tactics, then suddenly, we're onto something.

However, rather than always going for a 60/40 approach, perhaps consider a slightly more aggressive (but still safe) approach like an 80/20 allocation.

If stock markets look over bought (maybe assessed yearly), switch back to 60/40 or 70/30 particularly if the yields on bonds are high.

Just don't pay for someone to do this for you. It's utterly non-sensical/counterproductive!

You could buy FX, commodities, emerging markets, crypto, or the next great thing out there, or you could *buy global equities*.

Companies within these markets will take advantage of the latest craze for you. Betting on global stocks is like betting on the best and most innovative minds in the world.

If stock markets return 7 percent per annum on average, then as a foundation of your portfolio surely that's the place to be.

Spread your exposure between 6-7 of the major economies/markets with low-cost trackers, and you'll be doing a far better job than your IFA ever was.

Don't allocate too much in one direction (eg US tech) and spread your allocation between the UK (FTSE 100), Europe (DAX in Germany, CAC in France), Asia (Nikkei), and the US (S&P 500, Nasdaq and Dow Jones). Perhaps leave a small allocation for a slightly more emerging market. Maybe you believe Dubai is the next boom story? What about their Index? India? Consider theirs?

Once you commit, stick with your choices. Don't chop and change the mainstays as markets gyrate.

Like I said, it isn't rocket science.

With this market structure, you'll have the safety of bonds (established government bonds would be my suggestion), you'll have global exposure to the majority of stock markets, you'll be performing roughly in line with markets, you'll be diversified, you'll be receiving income and dividends, and you'll be ready to compound.

The lower fees alone make this a better structure.

Also, please also bear in mind that by buying global equities (stocks of the best companies in the world) you are also buying innovation. If any of the 'next great things' come into the mainstream, the companies who capitalise on the 'next AI' will be reflected in your holdings. You don't need to go looking for opportunities like this. They'll find you via your holdings.

<u>The above structure described is without incorporating some of our more sophisticated techniques discussed in this book.</u>

How you integrate them really depends on your risk appetite.

If the above (or similar) is your low-cost vanilla model, perhaps take 20 percent from the overall amount and set up an investment account utilising our three techniques as described. Or maybe even with two of the approaches and frameworks.

If you're slightly more aggressive, perhaps take 35 percent allocation (particularly if you steer away from our third more speculative technique).

Lower risk? Then how about 10 percent allocation?

Whatever route you decide to take and makes you comfortable, we expect the increased returns will boost your overall profits.

If you're generating 1.5 x your benchmark performance on 25 percent of your holdings, and matching general market performance on the rest, you're in a very sound place.

I expect it will be far better than any structure you've had previously.

How does 8 percent per annum sound v's 4 percent? 12 percent v's the 5 percent you've been receiving?

For the more speculative investors, you could have a larger portion of your portfolio exposed to our three techniques.

Ultimately, you need to make the choice.

In the investment world, we would always suggest starting slowly to get a feel for your new structure in both a rising and a falling market. Observe, test, tweak position size.

The world of wealth management is a simple one, and with the tools taught within this book you can build a better version of what you have or a structure with a few extra whistles and bells.

Make the call in regard to what works right for you and start your journey to market benchmark beating performance now.

The industry is evolving…. You need to do likewise.

We've covered a lot of ground in this book and as you can see, helping investors to improve their investment performance is a massive passion of mine.

Not only is it a great feeling for me to assist, but when you get this right, it has a profound impact on your life from here. It's ok for people to say 'money doesn't buy you happiness' (and in some respects they're right), but it certainly assists you to have a lifestyle without some of the stresses, and ultimately, a more enjoyable life.

Whether the extra portfolio gains assist you to fund a new business enterprise, buy a larger house, more freedom, perhaps pay your kids to go through school/college, pay off your parent's mortgage, or perhaps to give back via charity, it all becomes possible.

All the tactics and approaches brought to you in this book are provided to make you a better investor. Whether you only modify things slightly and it equates to an extra 2 percent per year, or you make wholesale changes, and they bring you 10 percent per annum, these returns quickly compound.

Everything in this book is designed to help you transition from a frustrated investor, into an investor who is regularly beating their market benchmark.

Do not be an investor who gets caught on the hamster wheel of underperformance and excuses. Do not get bogged down in the weeds like some of your peers.

Because if you do, those same stories of shame you hear from your wealth manager will be recycled for use year after year.

Being able to beat your market benchmark is the ultimate vehicle for creating the lifestyle you've always dreamed of.

We've been bred to believe that there is only one way to invest from a very young age; By friends and family, the media, and definitely the institutions, and over time it has chipped away at your beliefs and conditioned you to believe in them. Naysayers who have already thrown the towel in will continue to do what they've always done, but for you, change is coming.

I am telling you right now not to believe the doom and gloom mongers, don't believe an IFA who has never placed a trade in his lifetime, and who only has one goal, to earn fees from *your* money.

Making the right changes will create better relationships for you with your spouse, and with your kids. You'll have more capital to deploy in any manner of your choosing, whether you're buying multiple homes, the new sports car you've always had your eye on, properties for your children, putting your kids through school/Uni, holidaying 10 times a year, or all of the above! It is all possible if you make the changes required.

Society will lead you to believe that it isn't possible, that you should just do what everyone else does. I'm here to tell you to ignore them. This is a lie spread by people who haven't had the courage to make the change, who haven't manifested their dreams.

You can indeed have it all, and even if it's only a few extra percent per annum, every little counts.

On your transformative journey you will face challenges, you will face obstacles, and perhaps pressure. However, let me reassure you that to be successful, pressure will be a fact of life. The people who embrace it are the ones who succeed, the ones who become the high performers. These types of people are the ones who make hay whilst the sun is shining and forge ahead and make big strides, and when the chips are down. They fight, they tweak, they become better.

For high achievers, failure is not an option. There is no plan B.

As you're now close to the end of this book, there is a possibility that you might also have the ability to take on the challenges and thrive under pressure.

Making money in the markets isn't easy, beating them is even harder. Don't be fooled into thinking this book is your magic wand, that from today, everything will be easy. It won't. However, follow the principles outlined in here and you will make things substantially better.

Take your time, make the tweaks, and be rewarded.

As my daughters would say to their team mates on the netball court- 'You've got this'.

Chapter 19

FINALLY….

Although most of what I have learnt in my lifetime has been via trial and error, at times people have dropped some nuggets of wisdom into my arena or have opened a door for me.

Therefore, I am definitely of the opinion that if we can help others move forward like we're doing with this book, we should.

I'm trying to send the elevator down to you by writing this book, but in order for me to help more disillusioned investors just like you, I need word to spread first.

This is where you can come into it.

Once you've digested this book, once you've started to implement the learnings, and once you've started to make the tweaks on your portfolio, I have a small favour to ask

If you have found this book valuable, if it has helped you, helped you create the winning mentality, then please pass on the goodwill. Let your circle of friends, family and colleagues know about this book and leave a review for those coming up in the elevator underneath you.

It won't cost you a penny to do so, but it could empower another 10 frustrated investors just like you.

Every person we assist, every investor we help will make the industry a better place.

To leave a review- please head to the amazon bookstore and search for the book name.

Please leave a review on Amazon. It's greatly appreciated!

After you've done that, and if you're feeling super generous, you could also send a short review to any of the following:

Email lc@tppglobal.io

Text or WhatsApp 00 44 7782 382851

Thank you very much for taking the time out of your busy schedule to read my findings. Its people like you who motivate me to get up every day and make a difference to the world of investors.

I can't wait to hear about your results moving forward.

Get ready to change how you invest. Join the movement our strategies have been creating.

The investment revolution is underway.

BONUSES AND RESOURCES TO INSTANTLY CHANGE YOUR PORTFOLIO PERFORMANCE.

ABSOLUTELY FREE VALUE:

Bonus 1:

A lifetime of FREE market reports, insight, and analysis from the TPP dream team.

Scan the QR code below:

FREE market reports: Sign up.

Bonus 2:

FREE webinar training.

The three tactics that could assist you to beat your market benchmark.

Visit www.indexbeatinginvestingtpp.com and sign up.

Or scan the QR code below:

Bonus 3:

FREE demo portfolio traded by the masters.

Visit www.tppglobal.io or scan the QR code below to have access to four of the TPP strategies and watch how they perform in real time.

A must for any investor.

Bonus 4:

Link up with Lane Clark on Linkedin:

Linkedin profile:

Click here:

https://www.linkedin.com/in/laneclark/

Scan QR code.

Youtube account: https://www.youtube.com/channel/
UCG792Of08Aq611LYmlZUKWQ

QR code:

Lane Clark Blog. Read here:

Zero Hedge: https://www.zerohedge.com/contributors/355113

QR code:

Bonus 5:

FREE video regarding the three tactics disrupting wealth managers:

https://www.tppvideo.com/
book-your-strategy-call1723476547394

Scan QR code

Bonus 6:

FREE video explaining the one strategy EVERY investor needs. The leveraged tracker:

https://www.tppvideo.com/
book-your-strategy-call1723112465758

QR Code:

Bonus 7:

FREE video: The power of compounded growth:

https://www.tppvideo.com/
book-your-strategy-call1723476179710

QR Code:

Bonus 8:

FREE video: Why every investor needs to avoid these dog funds: AAAHHHHHH – These Blinking dogs haunt me!

https://www.tppvideo.com/
book-your-strategy-call1723476339019

QR Code:

Bonus 9:

FREE CONSULTATION CALL.

Book here:

https://testimonials.tppvideo.com/
book-your-strategy-call1717091666543

QR code:

Printed in Dunstable, United Kingdom

68816893R00107